WRESTLING
with Our
INNER
Angels

Faith, Mental Illness,
and the Journey to Wholeness

Nancy Kehoe

JOSSEY-BASS
A Wiley Imprint
www.josseybass.com

Published by Jossey-Bass
A Wiley Imprint
989 Market Street, San Francisco, CA 94103-1741—www.josseybass.com

Credits appear on p. 149.

Readers should be aware that Internet Web sites offered as citations and/or sources
for further information may have changed or disappeared between the time this
was written and when it is read.

Jossey-Bass books and products are available through most bookstores.
To contact Jossey-Bass directly call our Customer Care Department within the
U.S. at 800-956-7739, outside the U.S. at 317-572-3986, or fax 317-572-4002.

Jossey-Bass also publishes its books in a variety of electronic formats. Some content
that appears in print may not be available in electronic books.

Library of Congress Cataloging-in-Publication Data

Kehoe, Nancy, date.
    Wrestling with our inner angels : faith, mental illness, and the journey to
wholeness / Nancy Kehoe ; foreword by Russell Shorto. — 1st ed.
        p.   cm.
    Includes index.
    ISBN 978-0-470-45541-8 (cloth)
        1. Mental illness—Religious aspects.   2. Spiritual healing.   3. Spirituality.
4. Mental illness—Treatment.   I. Title.
RC489.S676K44   2009
615.8'52—dc22
                                                                    2009001143

Printed in the United States of America
FIRST EDITION
HB Printing   10 9 8 7 6 5 4 3 2 1

In Gratitude

To my parents for their faith, their love, and the example of their lives

To my brothers, Kim and Charles, who have journeyed with me

To all those who suffer with mental illness, especially those who have touched my life and been the inspiration for this book

Contents

Foreword

In 1997, when I was researching my book *Saints and Madmen: Psychiatry Opens Its Doors to Religion*, several therapists suggested that I interview Dr. Nancy Kehoe, a psychologist in Cambridge, Massachusetts, who was doing some innovative work with men and women in a psychiatric day treatment program. After an initial luncheon meeting, she invited me to be an observer at one of her groups. I was immediately taken with the way Nancy so adroitly used her dual identity—that of a Roman Catholic nun and a clinical psychologist. Without seeing it firsthand, I never could have imagined clients—some with quite complicated mental health issues—being able to address complex religious and spiritual questions. Nancy handled the complexities with remarkable respect and skill.

Now, in her own book, Nancy Kehoe invites us all in on her groups, to be observers and to listen with new ears and to see with new eyes, to look at men and women who have been so marginalized by their psychiatric diagnoses, and to wonder again at the resilience of the human spirit. What I did not appreciate about Nancy at the time I wrote the chapter in my book was how fully she has used her own life experience to identify with her clients, and how fully she has herself been open to change.

In today's world, when religious beliefs have become so divisive and the source of so much judgment and pain, Nancy Kehoe, in her life and her work, shows us that we can all be learners and teachers, that human encounters based on respect and openness can lead to healing. If psychiatry has opened its doors to religion, it is because people like Nancy have had the determination to keep knocking.

Whether you are a therapist, a client, a family member of someone who suffers with mental illness, or just someone who is curious about another person's journey, you will be affected by this remarkable book.

—Russell Shorto

Acknowledgments

I began this book with the hope of helping to change the face of mental illness. The faces that I encounter each week in the day treatment program have been my inspiration. When I thought of giving up, their support, their love, and their interest in this project kept me going. To them I owe my biggest debt of gratitude.

Over the years when I felt I was lost, wandering aimlessly on my journey, my mother would say to me, "Honey, you've got to have faith. I believe the Holy Spirit has something He wants you to do." For me, writing this book has become that "something." Almost from the beginning, I kept a list of all who helped me in some way, thinking that if my book was published, I would readily be able to acknowledge all those who helped me bring it to life. I am glad I kept the list.

This endeavor would never have come to completion were it not for three people: Anne Edelstein, my agent; Patricia Mulcahy, my personal editor; and Doctor Thomas Gutheil, my mentor, colleague, and friend. Anne believed in this project from the beginning, and her belief, her driving commitment to make it happen, her energy, her sense of humor, and her ability to instill hope in me when I had lost it kept me from sinking on more than one occasion. Patricia, a true teacher, worked tirelessly with me through draft after draft. Her humor, her experience, her liveliness, and her knowledge of the perilous world of publishing kept me on track. Tom, a friend and mentor for years, played a major role in helping me reframe the entire book. His intensity, his belief in me, his laser-sharp mind, and his innumerable gifts have been blessings for me.

Writing this book has been a journey in itself, and on this journey I have been sustained, nourished, supported, and encouraged by family members, members of my religious order, other writers, colleagues, and friends. My gratitude to each of them is profound, for it is very clear to me that I never would have accomplished this daunting task without each of them.

My brothers, Kim and Charles, have been like two compasses for me. Both are men of deep faith whose perspective on life and ability to see both the forest and the trees helped me find my path through the woods. My aunt and godmother, Frances Regan, has been a prayer partner from the beginning. My cousin Joan, who should be an editor herself, read and reread countless drafts and offered excellent critiques, as did my cousin Betty McGlynn.

My religious community—Sisters Jean Bartunek, Malin Craig, Gail O'Donnell, Meg Guider, and Susan Regan—have borne the brunt of this book for five and a half years. Without their love, support, encouragement, interest, and patience, it would have been almost impossible for me to persevere.

The members of two Provincial Teams—Sisters Kathleen Hughes, Ellen Collesano, Joan Gannon, Sheila Hammond, Paula Toner, Marina Hernandez, Kathleen Conan, and Anne Byrne—literally and figuratively supported my writing the book. In addition to the community in which I live, the Religious of the Sacred Heart in the Boston area have been my cheerleaders. The retired sisters in my community who live in Menlo Park, California, and in Albany, New York, have followed me with their prayers and their interest. In particular I am indebted to Sisters Maribeth Tobin, Mary Ranney, Gabrielle Husson, and Claire Saizan.

When the book was only a fantasy, I was initially helped by Kathleen Hirsch, Anne Bernays, and Justin Kaplan, who thought the idea had merit and encouraged me to pursue it. I am grateful they didn't elaborate on the perils of the journey. Cathy Switzer generously helped me with the initial proposal. Without her assistance, I never would have gotten to first base. Russell Shorto gave me the best gift of all when he put me in touch with Anne Edelstein, who brought Patricia Mulcahy into the loop. Thanks to a serendipitous meeting between Anne Edelstein and Sheryl Fullerton from Jossey-Bass, this book fell into the perfect hands. Sheryl grasped the essence of the book immediately and has been its champion ever since. Her enthusiasm for the project and her dynamic spirit have been an unexpected gift at the end of this journey. The staff at Jossey-Bass and at Wiley—Alison Knowles, Carrie Wright, Joanne Clapp Fullagar, Erin Beam, and Keira Kordowski—have been stellar. I have been fortunate to work with such gracious and dedicated men and women.

Friends and colleagues read and reread drafts. Each time it was like tasting a new dish with a kitchen full of experts: one suggested a little more salt, another a little less; some wanted more spice; and some just wanted the bare bones. Sisters Elizabeth White, Hilda Carey, Pam Hickey, and Mary Ann Flynn and my friends and colleagues Doctors Elissa Ely, Ana-Maria Rizzuto, Robert Levin; Mary Helen O'Hanley, Kathy Church, Inge Hoffmann, and Jane Raye have all made significant contributions to this text. Other friends, Father Jack O'Callaghan, Father Paul Lucey, Ellen Snee, Bessie Chambers, Al O'Hanley, Vito Notaro, Pat Lussiano, and Bob and Carol Coutu, as well as members of my book club Rosemary Hintereggen, Alice O'Halloran, Valerie Schmergel, Marjorie Sayer, Marie McDermott, Berely Tuttelman, Agnes O'Brien, Beth Jenkins, Charlotte Devoe, Judy Castaldi, and Rachel Spector, tracked the weekly, monthly, and yearly progress of the book.

Sister Margaretta Flanagan, Kiiko Matsumoto, and Jim Dolan kept my soul and body strong with their guidance and their gifts of healing.

During the ten years I worked with the Milwaukee Behavioral Health Division, I became more and more convinced that the spiritual lives of individuals with mental illness must be nourished. I owe Doctor John Prestby, the clinical director of the day treatment program my heartfelt gratitude for bringing me to Milwaukee and giving me the opportunity to work with his staff and "spread the word."

Some friends offered me their summer homes, giving me the opportunity to write in places of beauty and solitude: Molly Noonan and Barbara Sullivan, Elaine O'Reilly and Ron Benham, Joan and Peter Wrenn, and especially Diane and Ed Lowenstein.

For years my affiliation with the Department of Psychiatry at the Cambridge Health Alliance has been a rich source of educational and clinical opportunity for me. I am grateful to Doctors Jay Burke and John Mack for their support; sadly the latter's untimely death several years ago has deprived me of celebrating this achievement with him.

As on any journey, along the way we have chance encounters, interact with people briefly, and are touched in unexpected ways. For all the people I have met, too numerous to name, I am also deeply grateful.

Prologue

One fine spring day in 1981, as I dashed out the door, already late for an appointment, I heard the phone ring and impulsively decided to pick it up. It was a phone call that changed my life.

The director of a psychiatric day treatment program affiliated with one of the Harvard Medical School's teaching hospitals was requesting a consultation. When psychiatric hospitals were downsizing in the 1970s, day treatment programs were created in order to integrate patients back into the community. Staffed by mental health professionals, the programs offered group and individual therapy.

A nun since the age of eighteen, I am also a clinical psychologist who had a private practice for twenty-three years. After ending my psychotherapy practice, I began to do private consulting and training. Since 1980 I have been a clinical instructor in psychology at the Harvard Medical School. After finishing my doctorate at Boston College, I did a postdoctoral internship in the psychiatry department of one of the Harvard teaching hospitals. Since I didn't want to deal with potentially negative projections, only a few members of the psychiatry department knew I was a member of a religious order. I developed my clinical skills while quietly observing the fact that no one ever mentioned religion in relation to a client—for me, an intriguing omission. As I began to feel more clinically secure, I questioned the omission.

The day I answered that all-important call, little did I realize that I was about to address a deeply embedded psychiatric fear about the relationship of religion to mental illness. In the Boston-Cambridge psychiatric community, I was becoming recognized as "an interpreter," a person who could translate the foreign language of religion for therapists as they worked with clients who "did God talk." The director of the day treatment program described the dilemma to me on the phone: a Lutheran client was staunchly resisting therapy. He believed he could not work with his devout Jewish therapist, for she did not share his beliefs. He wanted her to convert to Christianity, a request she could not grant. The director hoped I could resolve the impasse.

The entrenched belief in the mental health community then was that therapists could not and should not talk about religion with "crazy people." A great divide existed, one I was about to help bridge, albeit inadvertently.

The day of the consultation was hot and humid. The June heat outside was in sharp contrast to the chilled, tense atmosphere I encountered when Clare, the director, introduced me to Donald, a tall, blond, well-built young man, and his therapist, Sara, short, thin, dark-haired, and attractive, with a kind face and intense, gentle brown eyes.

"This is Dr. Kehoe, who is also a Catholic nun," Clare said. "We have invited her to meet with you both, hoping that she might help you resolve issues that are interfering with your therapy."

Sara ushered us into a small room, a tight space for a conversation I felt would benefit from a little more distance between our three sets of knees.

Donald began with a question that has resonated throughout my career and one that has been at the heart of my own journey: "What shall I call you, Doctor Kehoe or Sister Kehoe?"

Although I felt pretty sure which of my professional identities he was going to recognize, I said, "Which would you feel more comfortable with?"

"Sister Kehoe."

"Fine," I said. "And you, Sara?"

"I'd like to call you Doctor Kehoe. I don't know any nuns."

There we were: one was allied with my religious identity and the other with my psychological one. I felt like Solomon facing the two mothers who each claimed the baby as her own. Clearly, Donald saw me as an ally who might help in the conversion process, two against one; Sara saw me as a clinical psychologist who could help Donald agree to work with her despite their religious differences.

With marked intensity, Donald said, "I am Lutheran and have been a divinity school student for the last two years. I don't have a mental illness, but I have been under a lot of stress with my academic work and some family issues. I ended up here because my roommate was worried about me."

As Donald spoke, I could see that he was adamant about the place of religion in his life, a position that would almost certainly be interpreted by most mental health professionals as a defense; they would say he was using religion to deny his illness.

When he paused, Sara said, "Donald wasn't sleeping, and his inability to concentrate meant that he wasn't doing well in his studies. The dean at the divinity school recommended a medical leave of absence."

I noted to myself that pressured speech, sleeplessness, and an inability to concentrate all suggested a more serious diagnosis than "stress."

Donald continued, "I like Sara, but then I found out that she is Jewish. I can't work with her because she is not a Christian. I have read a lot of Freud. I know what therapists think of people who have religious beliefs; they think they are sick or that they should grow up and let go of their childish beliefs. My religion means everything to me."

"Donald, I know that your beliefs are important to you," Sara replied warmly.

To me, Sara was an exception to the rule, for she recognized Donald's beliefs and seemed willing to work with them.

"But you don't believe what I do," Donald retorted.

Faced with Donald's forceful response, I said, trying to remain calm, "Donald, it sounds to me as though you fear that unless Sara converts to Christianity, she will try to take your beliefs away from you or that she will see them negatively."

"That's it, Sister Kehoe," Donald said. "I think that she is sitting there, thinking I am crazy because I believe in Jesus Christ, that I pray, that I ask God for help, even now. I have read a lot; I know that is what shrinks believe."

Sara intervened reassuringly: "Donald, I have my beliefs, but that doesn't mean I can't understand what yours mean for you and how they help you."

The sincerity with which Sara spoke and the compassionate look on her face made Donald pause. A moment of silence followed.

I added, "Donald, I hear a lot of fear in you. I sense that with all the stress in your life, you are afraid that Sara will take away the one thing that has been and continues to be a firm foundation for you. Can you believe that she can work with you, respect your beliefs, and understand how they help you without her becoming a Christian?"

Donald stopped, looked at Sara, and said, "Is that true? That you won't try to take my beliefs away from me? We can talk about them and about other stresses in my life?"

Sara responded sensitively, "Let's see if you feel safe when you talk about your beliefs. You can let me know."

By telling Donald that he should trust his own sense of her respect for him, Sara was building an alliance with him, thereby allowing room for the discussion of religion, a critical and uncommon position at that time.

Aware that some accord had been reached, I encouraged Donald to give therapy with Sara a chance, since she clearly understood his beliefs, even if she didn't necessarily share them.

In a more subdued voice, Donald agreed to try.

After they both thanked me, I offered to return at some point if they thought it would be useful.

When I met with the staff to debrief the session, to my bewilderment, they said that many clients referred to religion, but the therapists simply ignored it, not knowing how to handle the topic. This was an amazing admission for mental health professionals, who are trained to explore every aspect of a person's life, from the most intimate areas, such as sexuality, finances, and abuse histories, to the most public, such as work histories. Listening to, making sense of, and helping a person reframe the narrative of his or her life is the essence of therapy.

This conversation, however, suggested that the chapter that concerned religion was being omitted: the whole story could never be told because no one wanted to listen. The image that came to mind was that of archaeologists on a dig, unearthing sacred artifacts and tossing them aside because they were focused solely on certain aspects of a culture.

Having worked at a Harvard teaching hospital for five years, I had thought that the omission of religion in a clinical context was limited to that particular psychiatry department, given that religion was never mentioned in case conferences, evaluations, teaching conferences, or treatment dispositions. While training as a clinician, I never encountered overt resistance, but I always felt that the staff would rather have me at their bedsides if they were dying rather than at their parties. I had to keep knocking on doors to be included in conferences, even those focused on topics such as suicide. Now I was encountering a similar phenomenon in another system.

Over time I became aware that ignoring religion in a treatment context or seeing it as a part of a person's illness was the prevailing modus operandi in mental health work in this country. In the 1990s, as I began to offer presentations from Oregon to California, from Louisiana to New York, from Nebraska to Massachusetts, I learned that in general, clinicians did not explore a client's religious history. A quote attributed to Thomas S. Szasz, a Hungarian psychiatrist—"If you talk to God, it's prayer; if God talks to you, you're crazy"—captures this long-entrenched belief.

A Gallup poll conducted in July 2008 found that 78 percent of respondents expressed a belief in God, 15 percent expressed a belief in a Higher Power, and only 6 percent said they don't believe in either. In 1992 a similar poll found that 71 percent of Americans had a religious affiliation of some kind. During the 1980s, the figure varied between 67 and 71 percent. One out of four Americans suffer with mental illness. Yet in the 1980s the approach to treating adults with mental illness did not include any exploration or discussion of religion.

It wasn't always this way. Until the late eighteenth century, the interpretation and healing of illness were linked with religion but were not separated from the science of medicine. In the Bible, illness was linked with personal or family sin. In Greco-Roman times, the sick came to temples such as that of Asclepius, seeking a cure. Even "mad" people were brought to the temple.

In medieval times and later, demons were thought to cause mental illness, but natural explanations were also offered. Science, medicine, and religion were all seen as contributing to the process of healing. Toward the end of the seventeenth century, an unwritten social contract developed, separating the territories of religion, science, and government.

By the latter part of the nineteenth century, thanks to a growing emphasis on scientific methods, the emergence of professional schools, and the separation of psychology from philosophy, a clear separation between the mental health disciplines and religion was developing. Religion was considered unscientific, while medicine and psychology were esteemed as the "hard" sciences, branches of learning that were verifiable by scientific methods.

Because of Sigmund Freud's unparalleled influence on the way psychodynamic training and mental health treatment have been practiced in this country since the early twentieth century, his views on religion have been profoundly formative. Essentially, he viewed religion as a symptom of immaturity or pathological disorder. (The historical material has been drawn from Harold Koenig's work.)[1] Until the most recent edition of the Diagnostic Statistical Manual (DSM-IV), the official guidebook for the diagnosis of psychiatric disorders, all the references to religion were negative; they were seen as symptoms of illness.

With her groundbreaking and revolutionary book *The Birth of the Living God: A Psychoanalytic Study*, Ana-Maria Rizzuto brought God into the psychoanalytic community.[2] In what has become a classic, translated into five languages, Rizzuto explores the rich psychic material embedded in the way a patient represents God to himself or herself. She addressed and challenged the academic community, and I brought the influence of her work into the trenches.

In addition to having historical roots, the omission of the discussion of religion in treatment is also related to the fact that mental health professionals have higher rates of atheism and agnosticism than the general population. In their oft-cited 1990 survey, Bergin and Jensen found the following rates of atheism or agnosticism among clinicians: clinical psychologists, 28 percent; psychiatrists, 21 percent; clinical social workers, 9 percent; and marriage and family therapists, 7 percent. This survey also found that while professional rates of conventional religious preferences were found to be lower in some respects among mental health professionals than those of the public at large, there were nonetheless a significant number who said they had some investment in religion.[3] Eight years later, Waldfogel, Wolpe, and Shmuely surveyed 121 residents in five psychiatric residency programs and found that this group appeared to be more religious than reports from other studies of psychiatrists' religious beliefs. However, the size of the Waldfogel study limits its significance.[4]

Nevertheless, whether mental health professionals had a personal investment in their religious tradition, had left it, or never believed, they ignored it when it came to their clinical work.

After a presentation I gave at a conference on suicide, a well-known psychiatrist who has done extensive work on suicide told me, "When I was an adolescent, I closed the door on religion, and now you have come along and knocked on it." He wasn't grateful.

In keeping the door closed, he continued to disregard the role of religious beliefs in individuals considering suicide.

Currently, the role of religion pervades political discourse in this country, as does the separation of church and state. Twenty-seven years ago, though, in settings funded by state, county, or national governmental agencies, the understanding of the separation of church and state simply meant that there would be no discussion of religion at all. Thus for the last hundred years, Freud's negative interpretation of religion, the absence of training in professional schools, the disaffiliation of many mental health professionals from their religious traditions or their agnostic or atheistic positions, the fear that a discussion of religion was tantamount to proselytizing, and concerns related to the separation of church and state accounted for the complete omission or denigration of anything related to religion in a clinical context.

On the day of our staff meeting at the day treatment center in Massachusetts, the ghosts of this historical development were tangibly present as we reflected on the consultation I'd done with Sara and Donald. Having heard that staff ignored clients' references to religion and being convinced that the exploration of this part of a person's life could be clinically relevant, I proposed the formation of a group focusing on religious and spiritual beliefs. I saw this simply as an opportunity for the clients to talk about how their beliefs helped them as they dealt with their illness or whether their beliefs were a source of conflict.

To me this did not seem like a revolutionary idea; but the staff's response was a stunned silence. The first person to speak said in a horrified voice, "A group focusing on religious beliefs? We have never talked about that with individuals—to say nothing of doing it in a group."

Another voice chimed in: "That could be a disaster. Clients like Donald would try to convert all the other clients. He is a very forceful person, and many of the clients are very vulnerable, fragile people."

Someone else added, "I am afraid that Esther, who can be delusional already, would have her delusions affirmed. It would be like saying her delusions are valid."

In an agitated voice, another staff member jumped in: "What if the clients started asking us about our beliefs? I don't know what I would say."

The associate director concluded, "This could create a huge split in the community between those who took part in the group and those who didn't, and between the staff and clients, if the clients felt the staff didn't want to talk about this."

Finally, someone said, "What about the separation of church and state? We could lose our funding."

Fear, anxiety, hesitation, and resistance formed the staff's only response: no one could see any positive benefit to this idea.

Their reactions caught me completely off-guard. Because I was simply offering a suggestion, not advocating a project in which I had any particular investment at the time, I remained calm: "This idea can't be imposed, so perhaps you need to spend more time talking about it among yourselves, and let me know if you want to proceed." Subsequently I learned that the staff had actually toned down their reaction when I was present.

Ultimately, to my surprise, the staff hesitantly agreed to the idea. The highly respected director of the program offered to lead the projected group with me. Only later did I discover that she was the daughter of a Methodist bishop and had never felt free to discuss religion with clients because she had learned in her training not to broach this problematic topic. Yet her own religious background, her deep commitment to the well-being of the clients, and her willingness to take a risk ultimately persuaded the staff to give my proposal a try.

Intuitively I knew that I had to create guidelines so that potential problems could be contained. I wanted the groups to be interdenominational so that every client would feel welcome. The crucial guideline was that each member had to respect every other member and be able to tolerate differences in beliefs. Of all the directives, this was the most significant, and it has become the cornerstone, the commandment that we hold to religiously—no pun intended!

I made another rule for myself, one of inclusion. I did not want to be influenced by diagnostic categories and stereotypes. I never asked the nature of a person's illness, nor was anyone excluded because of a certain diagnosis, such as schizophrenia. Interest alone was the criterion for participation. Perhaps unconsciously, this came from my own experience of being stereotyped as a nun.

In initiating this project, I was not conscious of going down a path as uncharted and as unknown to me as the road my great-great-grandmother, Minnie White Kimball, a literal trailblazer in the early 1800s, took when she and her husband packed their belongings in a covered wagon, left New York, and joined the pioneer movement west. Like her, I was exploring new terrain, with no idea where the journey would take me. One difference between Minnie and me was that I was not part of a wagon train; mine was the only wagon.

Yet my journey has been no less eventful, though not in ways I ever could have anticipated. Over the years, I've been in therapy myself as I struggled with the meaning of my vocation. Living in a community of fellow religious in Boston, I had an ordered and full life, the years of spiritual struggle behind me. Or so I thought until my encounters with these remarkable people taught me to reexamine everything the church had ever taught me.

Although all the clients have given me permission to tell their stories, I have changed all names and identifying material to protect their confidentiality.

1

Exploring New Terrain

riving to the day treatment program for the first session, I knew the sweaty palms on the steering wheel of my yellow VW Bug were not due strictly to the heat and humidity: I was suffering from performance anxiety. The staff skeptics were waiting, ready to appear when the first client became delusional.

Earlier in the day, the clients had been told that a new group was to be formed, one focusing on religious issues, and that while all were welcome to join, they had the option not to.

On the way to the center, I managed to hit every red light. Waiting, I reassured myself that I would not lead the group discussion as a chaplain, or, for that matter, as a nun, but as a clinical psychologist who happened to be a nun. I had no idea about what I was to encounter, who the participants would be, or what ideas they might have about the group or especially about me. Maybe they'd had bad experiences with nuns.

That morning I had carefully chosen a soft yellow blouse and a yellow skirt with a blue pattern, simple earrings, and no cross or symbol of my religious affiliation. I did not want to look "nunny," nor did I want to appear off-putting in a too-professional way.

Up to this point, because I had not worked on an inpatient psychiatric unit, I had limited experience with clients suffering from serious mental illness. I recalled an incident in 1972 when I was attending a clinical pastoral education program at one of the state hospitals. Innocently walking onto the ward, I'd held out my hand to an elderly woman sitting in a chair in the day room.

"Good morning, I am Chaplain Kehoe."

In a flash, she swung her arm, hit me in the jaw, and said, "I don't want any g—damn chaplain talking to me!"

A decade later as I headed to another mental health facility, I knew I certainly wasn't going to introduce myself as "Chaplain Kehoe." Approaching the parking area, I saw only a slightly built woman in her fifties walking away from the house with her head and back hunched over, obviously carrying the heavy and unseen burden of depression. Anxiously, I noted that this was one client who was opting out of the first religious issues group. I hoped I wouldn't begin to see a stream of people leaving the building.

I parked my car, took a deep breath, said a quick prayer, and got out, trying to appear confident and relaxed as I approached the white structure, a pleasant facility that housed the program. A youngish-looking man came out, lit a cigarette, descended the stairs, and began walking in circles, totally unaware of my presence.

Though it wasn't far from the parking area to the house, I had already encountered two people off in their own worlds. While I mused on the sensation of being almost invisible, a woman with heavily made-up eyes, long earrings, a bright pink cotton blouse, a floral skirt, and laced boots, came out and said to me in a high-pitched voice, "So who are you?"

"I'm Nancy." I tried to sound calm, but my voice wavered.

"And what are you doing here?" She wasn't so much rude as curious.

"I am going to lead a group with some of the clients." I realized that I didn't want to use the words *religious issues* to describe the group. But she knew.

"Oh, you're the one that's going to do some religious thing."

"Well, I guess you could call it that. Are you going to come?" I asked hopefully.

"I'm thinking about it, but first I have to have my cigarette." Lighting up, she turned back to me and said, "You see, I have this rosary I wear around my neck—helps me at times."

"I hope you'll join us." I tried to be gracious, assuring her that I wanted her to participate.

"We'll see."

As I walked up the stairs and into the narrow corridor, I wondered if the woman with the rosary would ask me to say it with her or for her.

When I'd been in the house for the consultation a few weeks earlier, I had not paid much attention to the interior arrangements and what they suggested in relation to the psychiatric treatment offered there. To the right of the corridor were a kitchen and a dining area where some of the clients and staff were cleaning up after lunch. I discovered that preparing lunch, sharing a meal, and cleaning up were integral parts of the program. Dishes clanked; some clients chatted with the staff, and others wandered in and out.

To the left was the community room, where all the large meetings took place. An upright piano at one end, a sofa, an assortment of chairs, a file cabinet, plants, and scattered magazines made the room seem cluttered. Although the staff clearly made some attempt to make the room comfortable, it seemed to mirror the lives of the people who used it: like them, it was worn and tired, with a hand-me-down feeling.

The postures of the clients waiting for the religious issues group to begin suggested that life was a burden they struggled to carry and that they spent many hours waiting—waiting to be given their meds, waiting for groups, waiting for a cigarette break, waiting for lunch, waiting for a bus, in control of so little. In nice weather people could spend time outside. But in inclement weather the only place to congregate was in the community room or in the dining-kitchen area.

My palms were still sweaty as I went upstairs to the staff room to meet with the director, Clare. Because she was familiar with the clients, I knew I could depend on her knowledge and her expertise as we embarked on this new endeavor and I tried to get my bearings. Clare and the patients were in different groups together all week long: men's groups, women's groups, art groups, and substance abuse groups. I was the new kid on the block.

Together we went downstairs. As we entered the room and sat down, two clients joined the six already seated.

Clare began in a calm voice: "I'm glad you all are here. I'd like to introduce Nancy, who is a psychologist and a nun. She and I are going to run this group, which we are calling 'Spiritual Beliefs and Values.'"

We had decided on that name rather than "Religious Issues," fearing that any reference to *religion* might be problematic.

Clare continued, "The staff and I know that many of you have talked about your religion and your beliefs, but we haven't really addressed those topics in any way in your treatment. So Nancy has agreed to lead this group with me."

Her words sounded surreal to me. As I looked around the room at the eight participants, I choked up, because I saw men and women, aged thirty to sixty-five or so, who had been warehoused in state mental hospitals for years. My grandfather had been hospitalized twice for depression. As I sat there, flashbacks of painful visits with him washed over me. But the images passed quickly, and I refocused.

In the posture of the older clients I saw defeat. Life seemed to have gotten the better of them. The younger clients were more animated. One of the younger-looking men seemed to be having a conversation with someone unseen to the rest of us. Physical twitches and blank stares are telltale marks of psychiatric medications, and there was a lot of twitching going on. Many of the clients were overweight, a side effect of the meds as well as of years of poor institutional nutrition.

It dawned on me that I wasn't the only one taking a risk this day. In coming to the group, these men and women were risking a conversation about their religious views, views that might be termed delusional and might lead to stronger doses of medication. A total stranger, I was asking them to talk about their beliefs, a subject that may have been even more frightening than asking them to talk about sex or the use of drugs or alcohol.

Trying to sound calm, I said I was happy to be there and looked forward to having a chance to meet with them weekly. I asked them to introduce themselves individually and indicate what religious tradition they belonged to so that we could have a sense of one another's backgrounds, adding that it was fine for someone to be in the group who may not have come from a religious tradition of any kind.

One of the younger men in the group who was seated near the air conditioner said in a booming voice, "Can we turn the air conditioner off? I can't hear you."

After an animated discussion, we decided to leave it on. The two who had been having a cigarette break entered the room.

Clare said, "Alex and Jane, it's important for you to be here when the group begins, so next time you have to finish your cigarettes more quickly."

A woman named Betty said to me: "You're a nun. You don't look like a nun. Why don't you look like a nun?"

I felt challenged. Trying not to sound defensive, I replied, "Most nuns don't wear habits anymore."

Charlotte chimed in, "I saw a nun who looked like a nun last week. Some nuns still look like nuns."

I wondered if she wished I still looked like a nun.

"That is true," I told her. "Some nuns still do wear habits, but most don't."

Sheila said, "I wouldn't come to this group if you had a habit. I had nuns in school, and I hated them. They were so mean to me."

With some relief, I thought that I had one on my side, but I wasn't sure how Charlotte and Betty felt. So I said, "That is why we want to have this group, to give you a chance to talk about your experiences with religion."

I hoped we weren't going to spend all our time talking about bad experiences with nuns, "Sister Beatrice Marie who pulled my ears in third grade." But I kept this to myself and suggested to the group that we share our religious backgrounds.

Charlotte said, "I'm Catholic. I pray, but I don't know if God hears my prayers, because I have a mental illness."

Roger spoke next: "I'm a Pentecostal. I go to the Pentecostal church. I count on the Spirit to heal me."

Susan said, "I was a Catholic, but I'm angry with God because I had cancer and a mental illness. That's not fair—one's enough. So I don't want to talk to God."

With noticeable irritation, Betty said, "Is this just going to be about Catholics? I'm Jewish. I don't want this to just be about Catholics. Are you going to try to make us Catholics?"

Little did Betty know that having grown up in a predominantly Jewish neighborhood in Chicago, I cherished Jewish traditions. In my own way, each year, I observe the High Holy Days from Rosh Hashanah to Yom Kippur and celebrate Passover with my Jewish friends. At Hanukkah, I light my candles. On my knees, I begin and end each day with "*Baruch ata Adonai*," and I have a mezuzah at my door. My grandfather was Episcopalian. So I was bringing my own interdenominational history to the proceedings.

I tried to reassure her: "No, Betty, this is not just going to be about being Catholic. And I am certainly not going to try to make anyone anything. This is just about giving people a chance to talk about what they believe and to see how this group can help. As Susan said, she is angry with God. That is the kind of thing we can talk about. Have any of you ever talked about your beliefs with your therapists?"

"Are you kidding?" Netta said incredulously. "No, that's not safe. All those doctors would have thought we were crazy. I keep my beliefs to myself."

Donald explained, "I am Lutheran now, but I was a Catholic, and then I went to the Assembly of God. I don't have a mental illness. I just have a lot of stress in my life. I was in divinity school but had to drop out because of the stress."

Donald was the man who'd been trying to convert his Jewish therapist. Anxiously, I considered that he might now try to convert the group, since we had given him a forum for his beliefs. He might be a handful, I concluded.

Clare asked, "Hilda, what about you?"

"I'm nothing," Hilda replied.

"Did you ever belong to a religion?"

"As a child, we went to some church, but it didn't mean nothing to me."

Roberta joined in: "I don't believe in God, but I believe you have to have faith. I have faith. Faith is like a beacon. I write poetry. I'll bring in some of my poetry."

"That would be wonderful," I said. "I would love to hear it."

I explained the guidelines, and Clare ended the meeting— but not before Jane had the last word: "This is groovy," she said.

I suspect that everyone was on his or her best behavior that first day. Responses were limited and guarded, divulging only the most benign information, except for Susan, who had cancer, and Betty, who was concerned I had an agenda. I had a sense that they were testing me to see if I was going to defend God or if I thought it was OK to be angry with God, a theme that has cropped up again and again over the years. They were probing to see if I was really going to be neutral.

When I started the group, I secretly entertained a wish that the men and women in it would discover a kinder God, not the angry one they feared. In the early years of my own life as a religious, the God I had encountered seemed demanding and harsh. I, too, was looking for a gentler God, though I scarcely realized it at the time.

As each group member explained his or her background, it was evident that we had the potential for some lively discussions, as well as the possibility for tension; we were Roman Catholic, Jewish, Pentecostal, atheist, Methodist, Lutheran—a great diversity, with mental illness the only common denominator.

Back upstairs, Clare and I uttered a huge sigh. Our first group discussion had developed fairly organically, although this first attempt was a little like leading an orchestra in which everyone was playing from a different sheet of music. I was to learn that this would happen frequently.

In my journal that night I wrote only, "I began the Spiritual Beliefs and Values group at the day treatment program today." Clearly, I held no crystal ball to tell me the significance of that day or what the future held in relation to it.

After this initial meeting, new members joined, and a few dropped out. Over the years a core group of regular members has formed the backbone of the group, with others coming and going, due to hospitalizations, departures from the program, or the choice for a different group within the program.[1] Early on, I developed a pattern, always beginning by asking what was on people's minds that day. I could see that a certain confessional tone was emerging. Members would talk about not having gone to church for a long time or having an affair and feeling guilty. "Sister, forgive me . . . ," they'd begin. Some talked about "church shopping" and wondered if it was OK. They were testing what was kosher to say to a nun.

After the first few weeks, it became clear to me that I could stop making generalizations. I saw no need to have a planned program; I just showed up. While I usually came with some ideas that might focus the group, it seemed that the members had their own agenda. Fortunately for me, during the summer months and into the fall, Clare was a steady presence. Beneath my calm exterior, I felt anxious and insecure every week as I drove into the parking lot. Gradually I was learning how intense the sessions could become.

One day I began a session by introducing myself to two new members and telling them, "We ask each new person what religion you belong to and what brings you to the group," a fairly benign request that on this particular day unexpectedly unleashed pent-up emotions. Before the words were out of my mouth, one of the new members, a tall, thin young man with wavy red hair, neatly dressed in slacks and a sport shirt, said in a compressed tone of voice, "I'm Burt. I was raised Congregationalist, but I just think that it's important to believe in yourself—that you need to believe in the positive. I think that is related to believing in God. Clare, don't you agree that you need to believe in yourself?"

"I do, Burt," said Clare, "and I know that you struggle a lot with that."

"It is so important," Burt insisted, "to believe in yourself."

The repetition made me keenly aware of how desperately he wanted to believe in himself but didn't. Then we heard from the other new member, Matt: "I went to a Pentecostal church. But I know when I am getting manic that I can use religion in the wrong way. I really go overboard, so that is not a good sign for me. I do talk with my therapist about God, even though he tells me he is not a believer."

"But Matt," Donald responded, "religion is good for you. It is good for me."

I'd been waiting apprehensively for this side of Donald to appear. With what I hoped sounded like gentle firmness, I reminded him of what we'd said at the beginning: that this group was not about trying to convince people about our own beliefs but about listening to each person and hearing what his or her beliefs meant. Though Donald's religious beliefs and practices helped him, what Matt was telling us was that he recognized that getting too religious was for him a sign of becoming manic.

"You got that right, Nancy," Matt said.

Ricardo chimed in: "The Blessed Virgin protects me. You know, she appears to people. Do you think she will appear to me?"

"Ricardo, I am not quite following you," I said.

"Nancy," he replied, "you don't want to follow me; I'm lost."

At this, everyone smiled, and after a pause, Sheila spoke: "I don't always find God in church. I find God in people. I have been working for the Little Sisters, and I see their kindness. I see a change in me working there. I am gentler with myself. The sisters say that God does not push you beyond what you can do. I'm not sure I always believe that, because sometimes I feel pushed pretty far. Nancy, what do you think of that?"

For the first time I was being put on the spot. "I am not opposed to answering those kinds of questions," I said, "but I really think it is important to hear what each person thinks. I am not here as the expert to give answers but to help us all struggle with our questions."

I really meant that: I wanted to know how they made sense of this kind of religious message, a message that I, too, had heard often—that God doesn't give us more than we can bear. At that moment I didn't have time to process my thoughts about something I had uttered glibly in the past.

It struck me as a question with many layers, and I needed time to reflect on the lives of people burdened seemingly beyond their capacity. Questions such as Sheila's have made me reexamine much of what I've been taught as I've struggled with the clients to make sense of life, of suffering, of religious teachings.

Donald noted, "Scripture says that God tests those He loves," whereupon Netta burst in angrily, "What kind of a loving parent pushes their kids beyond their limits? I feel that is what God does to me sometimes—He pushes me beyond my limits."

I hoped Netta wouldn't demand an explanation from me: with her experience of parental abuse, mental illness, and losing a child to foster care, she has been pushed pretty far. Fortunately, Tonja changed the subject.

"What about God and forgiveness?" she asked. "I feel I have done things I can't be forgiven for. I didn't take good care of my kids, and now they are in foster care. I think that's a terrible sin, and I am being punished for it."

Charlotte chimed in, "I don't get this forgiveness stuff. How can Hitler be forgiven for what he did to all the Jews?"

Kerry seemed to concur: "I don't believe in God. If there was a God, how could He let the Holocaust happen? I have hope, but I don't have faith."

Over time I was to learn that Kerry often came back to the Holocaust, making me wonder if his obsessive-compulsive disorder (OCD), self-diagnosed while watching *The Oprah Winfrey Show*, was his own Holocaust. It had robbed him of his life. But at that moment I was overwhelmed as the discussion moved from believing in oneself to God's testing people, to punishment and forgiveness, to Hitler.

Matt joined the discussion: "And not just what he did to the Jews but to people with mental illness, like us, and to gay people and elderly people and Gypsies. How can God forgive Hitler?"

"Scripture says God will forgive over and over again," Donald pointed out.

"But aren't there things," Tonja interjected, "that are just too bad to be forgiven?"

And Charlotte said to Donald, accusingly, "You hide behind Scripture, but what about that? Do *you* think that Hitler can be forgiven?"

Charlotte was expressing exactly what I'd been thinking: don't just give us Scripture; tell us what you think.

Donald replied, "Scripture says God will forgive. Maybe I don't get it, but that is what it says, and I try to hang on to what it says, even when I don't understand."

Burt noted, "What I think is important is accepting the good in oneself. We have to find the good in ourselves, not just the bad. We have to believe in ourselves."

Wanting to acknowledge the validity of all these questions and feeling challenged by them, I said, "I think the question of forgiveness, especially in light of horrors like the Holocaust, is difficult to get our minds around."

Our allotted time had run out. Clare summed up: "Today we have talked about believing in ourselves, the question of forgiveness, where some of us find God, and how people use their beliefs—all rich topics that we can come back to. But we have to end for now."

Driving back to my office in my little yellow Bug, I reflected on the discussion. Does God hand us more than we can deal with? Would God forgive Hitler? Was Donald going to become a handful? But given that I had appointments immediately with my private psychotherapy clients, there was little time to dwell on the questions the clients had raised with such clarity.

Feeling that my life was stable and fulfilling, I went about the rest of my week. On a daily basis, I didn't feel pushed beyond my limits as these clients did, so it was less urgent for me to come up with a satisfactory response to their existential questions.

But at some point their questions seeped into me and changed me, the way rain changes land formations or rocks, a drop at a time.

One postcard-perfect New England fall day, the kind that always makes me glad to be alive, with a clear blue sky and leaves of gold and red tinged with green and orange, I saw the group in a new light. I am ashamed to admit that I, too, had some preconceived and to some extent unconscious negative notions about mental illness before meeting with the men and women in the program. It was group sessions such as the following that began to alter my perspective.

Outside, the air was clear, brisk, and invigorating: But for the clients, the interior climate was gray and somber. When I arrived at the group, I heard the news: one of the men who had been in the program the previous year had committed suicide at one of the residential houses.

When Clare and I entered the community room, the atmosphere was like that of a wake. A pall hung over the eleven clients present. No one spoke.

In a soft voice, Clare began: "I told Nancy about Jack's death and that many of you knew him."

Donald said, "His death makes me really sad."

Charlotte said, "I know I shouldn't feel this way, but I get angry when I hear that someone killed himself. I try so hard to hang on, and then someone goes and ends it all. I think—why couldn't he keep trying, like I do?"

Sheila said, "I have tried to kill myself more than once. When you get that far down and you feel so much pain, you just want to end it all. You can't imagine living another day feeling so bad."

Charlotte rebutted, "I have tried to kill myself, too, but now I am glad that I didn't succeed. I can see there is some light at the end of the tunnel."

Roberta admitted, "I tried to jump out a hospital window, but luckily someone saw me in time and stopped me. Now I am grateful that I didn't end it all. I wish I knew who saved me so I could thank him."

In my private practice I had clients who were suicidal at times, but I had never been with so many individuals in one place who had attempted suicide. Their pain, their memories of going to the brink, of not wanting to live another day with so much misery, the honesty of their response to Jack's death—it all moved me. They were not being dramatic; they were simply telling their stories and expressing their feelings with integrity, coherence, and clarity.

Never had I heard people being so honest about what they felt in the face of death, and I have been to a lot of wakes. At the time of this meeting, the brother-in-law of a friend of mine was dying. No one would talk to him about his impending death, nor would family members talk to each other. I had worked with clients whose family members committed suicide who lied about the cause of death for years. Thus the openness of the group members touched me deeply.

Roger spoke up: "What is so terrible is what happens to the people you leave behind. My father killed himself, and our family has never gotten over it."

Kay added, "Pain sucks. You just aren't yourself. You just want to get rid of it, and it goes on and on. At that point, you aren't even thinking clearly."

"At those times," I asked, "does it feel like you can't connect to anything, to anyone, or to any beliefs that you might have?" I was struggling myself, trying to grasp the level of their pain.

Donald asked if it was true that the Catholic church says you will go to hell if you kill yourself.

I'd been dreading this question because in fact the Catholic church had changed its teaching on the subject. Suicide used to be deemed a mortal sin, and the person could not have a Mass or Christian burial. Indeed, it was the fear of hell that seemed to have kept some people from killing themselves. But the church's teaching had changed, and suicide was no longer considered a mortal sin.

Though I was worried that telling the truth might be a factor in someone's suicide, I decided to take the risk and trust that each person could deal with it. That decision—to tell the truth even when it seems potentially problematic—has continued to shape my responses to the clients over the years. This day was the first test.

I told them that though the church used to teach that suicide was a mortal sin, it now recognizes that a person in that much pain is not fully himself or herself.

Sheila added, "I have known both physical pain and mental pain, and I think mental pain is worse."

I asked, "How do we tap into any faith when we are in so much pain?" Feeling powerless in the face of their comments, my question seemed weak and ineffectual.

"Sometimes knowing others care helps," Sheila explained.

"That is when I go to Scripture," Donald said.

As we ended this painful session, Clare put on her clinical director's hat and reminded the group that if anyone was feeling particularly stressed, he or she should contact her or one of the other staff members.

Later Clare reflected on the fact that these patients in the Spiritual Beliefs and Values group handled the discussion of suicide very differently from members of other groups. Although they shared their own experiences, the focus was not on whether people felt safe, as it was in other groups when the issue of suicide came up. To Clare, it seemed that the members connected more deeply with each other in our discussion and really heard each other's anguish. Empathy, a heartfelt connection among the group members, rather than the clinical assessment of safety, seemed to make all the difference.

I found it difficult to open myself up to that much suffering. Though I spent the rest of that beautiful day trying to walk in the clients' shoes, at that point I just wasn't equipped to do it. It would take me years of listening to the group members, as well as a personal experience of depression, before I reached a deeper level of understanding.

More than two years after I began the group, I faced another challenge the day Peter joined. Occasionally, the members had talked about their religious delusions, but they never came to the group in the grip of one. During one session, three shared, quite humorously, the times they were John the Baptist and tried to baptize innocent passersby.

Then Peter showed up, sat down, and asked me if I believed he was Jesus Christ. I tried to explain the nature of the Spiritual Beliefs and Values group to him, but he didn't want an explanation. He just wanted me to confirm his new identity.

Finally I said, "Peter, I am not qualified to answer that question. But maybe today is not a good day for you to be in the group." Arguing with a delusion is a no-win situation, so I invited Peter to leave and return the following week, which he did, this time with his delusions under the control of medication. This was one of a very few instances in all the years I have led the group that I was asked to believe that Jesus was there in the room with me.

Reflecting on this session, I think I made a mistake. I was afraid. I had not yet encountered someone with an active delusion. I didn't want Peter to disrupt the group. Now that I have more experience, I wish I had engaged him in a conversation, trying to understand if he felt burdened, reminding him that "being Jesus Christ" means that a lot is expected of you. I know now that Peter was trying to tell me something, but I didn't hear him.

Many years later I was able to use my experience with Peter when a member of another group said she was a Wiccan. Rather than being driven by my discomfort and ignorance of what it meant to be a Wiccan, I was able to ask how she came to that belief. The group members and I learned that she was gay; since her religion taught her that being gay was a sin, she sought out a group of women that accepted her.

Two years after beginning the first group, I was asked by another clinical director to form a similar one at another psychiatric day treatment program. The two programs served the same population of clients, men and women who suffered from serious mental illness. In 1983 I started the second group with a little more experience and more openness on the part of the staff. For six years, from 1983 to 1989, I also led two groups at one of the Massachusetts state hospitals.

Not being a permanent member of either program, I came in each week as an outsider. Once a week I would drop into the two programs, lead the groups, and leave; this was a safe, detached position. For a long time I had a "we-they" mentality. As one of the "healthy" staff, I, the professional, was helping the "unhealthy."

Looking back, I can see the change in me, though I can't name the time or the place when the tide shifted. But I know I have become, in the words of one of my patients, "an honorary mental patient."

With a track record of 3,224 group sessions, I can attest to the fact that no client has ever become more delusional because of the group, no client has tried to convert others in the community, and no client has resisted working with a therapist of a different belief. Clients with different religious beliefs have not split the community. These twenty-seven years have uncovered a rich inner terrain, one that had been hidden from mental health providers but has been a source of strength and resilience for the clients.

This book is my attempt to bear witness to the stories of some of the remarkable men and women I have encountered in these programs: the lessons we can learn from them, what they have taught me, and how I have been changed by their presence in my life as I grapple with the true meaning of the spiritual. In a world with so many burdens to bear, those who have borne theirs with so much grace and dignity and resilience have much to teach us all.

2

Beverly's Quest

When Beverly joined Spiritual Beliefs and Values in the summer of 1985, I was still grappling with the purpose and significance of the group. For her it was an opportunity to talk about her religious beliefs, something she had never done in the forty-five years she'd spent in the mental health system.

Though she was one of the most articulate members of the group, Beverly irritated me with her self-deprecating posture, which seemed disingenuous. When addressing the others, she expressed compassion and sensitivity, often encouraging them to trust God, to turn to Him, and to see the good in themselves. But when referring to herself, she focused primarily on her sense of shame and guilt, her "badness."

After a session, she would often ask me if I thought she was evil. Never realizing the depth of the anguish that prompted the question, I assured her that I didn't think so. At that time I knew nothing of her tumultuous psychiatric history. After she "graduated" from the day treatment program two years later, she kept in touch, sending me articles she was writing, offering me some of her poems to use in presentations, and writing letters about her desire to help people with mental illness believe in their spirituality.

One year, together with an associate pastor of Beverly's church, we made Christmas tree ornaments to be sold at the annual parish Christmas bazaar. The purpose of this creative endeavor was to bring together members of the parish and people with mental illness in an effort to break down stereotypes. Spurred on by the success of this event, we had a cookie bake in the spring. Beverly relished these opportunities to educate others.

Beverly always called me "Sister Nancy," something that really nettled me: I wanted to be Doctor Kehoe, not Sister Nancy. Yet in addressing me this way, I knew she wanted to identify with the religious person, not the shrink; she had enough of those in her life. At another level, I understand now that she was also inviting me to relate to her religious side, keeping her darker side hidden from me, lest I reject her, as so many other mental health providers had. While she was alive, I never encountered the darker, deeply disturbed side of Beverly, which I discovered only later in her writings and in conversations with some of her caregivers. In contrast to the deferential, self-effacing, almost childlike person she was with me, I found a tormented, highly manipulative, self-destructive, angry woman.

In 1988 she was diagnosed with breast cancer. For ten years she enjoyed a period of remission, but ultimately the cancer recurred. This time she knew it was terminal. In the last few weeks of her life, she was admitted to a hospice, where I visited her as she lay in a short-sleeved hospital gown. Her arms looked like sheets of lined paper, line after line of scars, of self-mutilation, each one a cry for help. Seeing the evidence of all this pain, I could only wonder at the journey she had taken to achieve inner peace. As I said my final good-bye, I had no notion of the way she would come to influence me.

Later that week about fifty people gathered at a memorial service to honor and remember her in a large, open room in the halfway house where Beverly had spent the last five years of her life. This was not a meticulous, well-appointed funeral parlor but rather an awkward space with an odd assortment of mismatched, battered furniture, symbolic, in a way, of the women and men who inhabited the house. Sadness and affection marked the gathering. The warm April day, with its suggestion of new life, lent a spirit of hope to the event and paid tribute to the resilience of this complex woman.

Pictures of her spread out on a table at one end of the room showed a different Beverly, not a woman ravaged by cancer and mental illness: Beverly as a child playing with her brother; Beverly as a beautiful college student, fair-skinned, with wavy blond hair; Beverly on vacation with friends, happy and carefree, the "all-American girl." But no one in this gathering had known *that* Beverly—the attractive girl who seemed to have everything: friends, good looks, and education.

What few had seen was the other Beverly, the determined spiritual seeker, a woman hidden beneath the covers of the materials assembled near the photos: her journals and her books on spirituality, the mystery of suffering, depression, AA, and self-help, pointed elsewhere. Every person in the room, both caregivers and clients, had been enriched, challenged, enraged, engaged, and saddened by Beverly, whose lively intellect, literary gifts, and generous spirit were a blessing. At the same time, burdened by her mental illness, she had been a maddeningly difficult subject for the many therapists with whom she had worked.

As everyone settled in for the service, Lucy, Beverly's best friend and housemate, rose to say a few words. "We all called her Bev. This past Christmas, she was taking a math course. She received only three hundred dollars a month from Social Security's disability insurance. Since she didn't have enough money to buy Christmas gifts, she knitted socks for each woman in the house. When I had to go to the hospital, she would always go with me in the ambulance, so I wouldn't have to go alone. She believed very strongly in God and wasn't afraid to die."

Each person at the service testified to Bev's kindness, her generosity, and her keen, inquisitive mind. One described how she studied a stack of French and English vocabulary words as she smoked. Another referred to her love of literature and math, as well her own poetry. Some spoke of her overwhelming depression and self-loathing; others recalled times when her acute sensitivity to the tone of another caused her to burst into tears at one cross word, like a gravely wounded child.

But among these reflections, scant reference was made to the essential quest in Beverly's life—her relentless desire to understand the difference between her psychological symptoms and what was happening to her spiritually. Despite everything she'd shared both in the Spiritual Beliefs and Values group and in our subsequent conversations, I had little inkling of her inner struggles.

A week after the memorial service that touched me so deeply, the director of the halfway house called to say that Beverly had willed me all her journals and her modest library. By accepting this legacy, I was unsuspectingly establishing a whole new posthumous relationship with her, one that would ultimately inspire me to write about people who are so much more than their illnesses.

The following day I went to collect the "estate" I had inherited: a shopping bag of forty books, a blue plastic crate stuffed with twenty-five spiral notebooks, and reams of loose papers. Most of the material was torn and weather-beaten. Knowing that Beverly had spent years in the mental health system, I was amazed that she had somehow managed to keep all of this material. I resented the fact that in entrusting me with her writings, she was giving me the message that I was to "do something" with them. Her life was not to be discarded. At one point, she and I had talked of collaborating on a book, but one of my colleagues forewarned me that such an endeavor could be fraught with difficulties. In her own uncanny way, in death she was still inviting me and challenging me to write a book "with her."

As I began to read through her journals, I noted right away that she focused on the here and now; references to her early history were notably lacking.

To fill in some of the missing pieces of her life, I interviewed some of her former therapists. The more I learned about

Beverly, the more I grasped the extent of the damage that had been done to her because her providers had explored neither the religious and spiritual dimension of her life nor her creative side. Her determination to pursue a spiritual quest, so evident in her journals, can only be fully appreciated by understanding the path of her illness.

Beverly grew up in a rural area of New Jersey. Both her brilliant, but possibly psychotic, father and her mother abused her sexually and emotionally. An older brother—who later deprived her of her inheritance—also participated in the abuse. School was a safe haven, the place where she excelled and was respected. Until her death, her intellectual pursuits were a stabilizing force.

Although she always resisted thinking of herself as a trauma victim, her drawings done as an adult in expressive therapy groups suggested this history. One dark and ominous picture of a house was titled "House of Horrors." In another, a girl sits with a man standing over her, presumably her father. Titled "Rewards," the picture shows fifty cents for a C grade, twenty cents for a B, and ten cents for an A: a sadistic way to control a clever child.

In one of her essays, titled "My Self-Story," she refers to being hospitalized at age eleven for depression and anxiety. This was in 1946, when psychiatric institutions were aptly designated as "snake pits" and therapists rarely explored issues of child abuse. Years later with one of her therapists, Beverly recalled thinking, *No one will believe me. I am bad, and I can't let anyone see me.* At the time of her hospitalization, she was seen as the problem, and therapists tried to modify her bad behavior and morose moods.

It was horrendous to imagine a pretty eleven-year-old in a locked hospital ward in 1946, probably surrounded by unkempt adults pacing the room talking to themselves or to their voices or squatting in fetal positions. In those days, there was no art therapy or play therapy by which a child could communicate nonverbally. After the horrors of the first hospitalization, Beverly decided to "keep it together," which she did until she went to college: She played the game of "wellness" to perfection.

After the dramatic transition from rural New Jersey to one of the large state universities in Florida, she started to suffer from major mood swings, involving depression and bouts of suicidal feelings. The latter escalated when another student killed herself, and Beverly "broke down." At this point she began her lifelong sojourn in the mental health system.

In one of her journals she summarized her tormented journey: "Until three years ago, my emotional history was bleak and, to me at least, shameful and extremely embarrassing. This is not to say I did not have my measure of good times, a few successes, and intermittent periods of what I now believe were God-given feelings of hope and joy. But the prognosis was generally poor, the pain exquisite, the failures and self-sabotaging continual—and the relationship to God and others, severely impaired."

Beverly wrote this at age fifty-six, after forty-five years of hospital admissions and a ten-year incarceration, mostly in state hospitals. She was given numerous neuroleptics, antidepressants, tranquilizers, and mood stabilizers and received fifty-three ECTs (electroconvulsive treatments), generally given without anesthesia, as well as insulin shock.[1] She indicated that except for a four-year period in the early 1970s, the psychotherapy she received was ineffective or downright damaging. The many conflicting diagnoses she was given were a great source of terror and guilt. As she put it, she felt "terminally unique" (an AA term). "I could not be appropriately categorized and thought myself a spiritual and emotional anomaly."

In those years psychiatric medications were less effective than they are today. Each additional piece of research offered the potential for a new diagnosis and new medications. Beverly's diagnoses included major depression with psychotic features, borderline personality, schizoaffective disorder, and bipolar illness, all of which defined her at one time or another. In those years the concept of recovery from such diseases was unknown. Mental illness was a life sentence.

At the time of her second emotional breakdown at age nineteen, Beverly was astute enough to make this assessment: "Good state-of-the-art treatment was virtually unknown in Florida, so I moved to New York, and my history of recurrent hospitalizations began." At first she was in a prestigious private hospital considered "second only to Menninger's" (a renowned psychiatric center in Topeka, Kansas), but she did very poorly there. She described being treated brutally, even scapegoated. Because she thought psychiatric personnel should be caring and benevolent people, she concluded that she was the problem; this seemed to be the origin of her belief that she was inherently evil. She could not see the staff as lacking, any more than she could view her family in that light.

At age twenty, totally lost and apparently alone, she was discharged prematurely from the private hospital and committed to a notorious state hospital nearby. Because of a morbid prognosis there and concern for her safety, after six months the staff transferred her to a maximum-security back ward, where she spent the next three years. With unabated anguish, she describes being in a constant state of depression. Miraculously, in these dire circumstances she met an astute, compassionate psychiatrist who put her on the drug Elavil.

On Elavil, Bev's life became a roller-coaster: for the next thirty years she experienced periods of stability and energy alternating with periods of depression, terror, and psychosis. In difficult times, by her own admission, she sabotaged her academic work, her relationships, her jobs, and her living situations and began cutting herself to make her pain credible to her caregivers. She was a "torn" woman, ripped apart by her longings to find care and love yet acting in such a way that she drove others away.

At some point she moved from New York to Boston. In one of the journals, she refers to working with caring therapists at a prestigious Boston hospital for four years. With their help, she gained some stability and graduated from college with high honors in 1976 at age forty-one, thirty years after her first hospitalization—a testimony to her determined spirit. But the degree did not alleviate her emotional pain.

She continued to act out, desperately trying to get the attention of caregivers, trying to find the loving parents she never had. She needed to have her pain recognized; at the same time, she alienated her caregivers with her manipulations, her obsequiousness, and her clever schemes, which took extreme forms at times.

Once she hid under the desks in the emergency room. If a wailing two-year-old can set people on edge, imagine what an overweight, desperate-looking, middle-aged "madwoman" having a temper tantrum at two in the morning can do to a beleaguered staff and other emergency room patients! In an act of desperation, she cut herself and received 119 stitches, but her suicidal gesture was not taken seriously, and the hospital refused to admit her.

The passages in her journals describing these escapades read like segments from the TV show *ER*. Shrewdly, she seemed to have a knack for choosing the busiest time for the hospital staff. One cold December night she went to an emergency room, frantically seeking care. After being told to leave, she eluded the guards and ascended to the roof of the hospital. She approached the edge, ready but afraid to jump. In her mind, the only way to get the attention she craved was to attempt suicide.

Tortured and torturing, she described it as follows:

> I knew the staff had to take a suicidal gesture seriously, so I
> got as close to the edge as I dared, knowing someone would
> come. The guard did, urged me to back away, showed alarm and

concern, and brought me back to the ER. For a few minutes I
received kind attention, but then the psychiatrist asked me if
I had really intended to kill myself and I had to admit that I
didn't. I knew how to manipulate the staff, but they hated me for
it, and that added to my sense of being evil, a devil.

For hospital personnel, Beverly was what they call a "frequent flyer," a psychiatric patient who kept returning, one whose name the staff recited with dread and loathing.

From a psychiatrist who treated her at that time I learned that one of her patterns was to go to the emergency room saying she was suicidal and get herself admitted to the inpatient unit voluntarily for a three-day stay, which often ended on Friday. Exhausted by the week, the residents had to assess whether it was safe to discharge her. She would feign a commitment to keeping herself safe, but they were often unsure of her sincerity. Fearing her suicidal tendencies, the staff would commit her to a hospital with a locked unit as Friday afternoon faded into Friday evening. The anger of the residents mounted as the clock ticked away, with another Friday evening lost on Bev, who apologized profusely for "taking so much time." The voluminous size of her charts tells the story of this pattern.

In the late 1980s, after a fifteen-month stay at one of the state hospitals, she was transitioned to a halfway house for the chronically mentally ill, a place that offered the potential for a new beginning. Although for the first time she felt she was in a safe, caring, and respectful environment, Beverly was still a victim of chronic depression and had periods when she acted out her pain and was hospitalized.

During one of these admissions, the pattern was broken by Janet, a psychology intern with no prior experience with Beverly. In Beverly's room Janet found a dumpy, grandmotherly looking woman with graying, shoulder-length hair sitting on a bed doing calculus. The intern told herself, *This woman has strengths*. Janet saw possibilities, not problems.

That was the beginning of a relationship that proved to be transformative for Bev as Janet connected with a side of her that had remained hidden from all her other caregivers. It was at this time that she was diagnosed with her first breast cancer. Thanks to this diagnosis and the new therapist, she received the care, concern, and attention she had longed for all her life. But it wasn't easy for her to forgo her old ways, to stop seeing herself as evil and deserving of harsh treatment. After discontinuing the Elavil, she became severely depressed, made a serious attempt on her life, and was hospitalized yet again—the ultimate wake-up call. After a short stay in the intensive care unit, she says, "I knew the greatest remorse in my life. God, in his mercy, showered me with forgiveness, new hope, and love. I vowed 'never again.' I would endure to the end."

And endure she did, until the second bout of cancer claimed her life but not before she came to a greater sense of freedom. In one journal entry she wrote, "No longer imprisoned by the crippling effects of isolation and self-hatred, I no longer walk alone—paradoxically, that makes me feel even closer to God."

In the Spiritual Beliefs and Values group and in the writings she shared with me while she was alive, she revealed something of her inner life. As I read the entries in the journals, I began to understand more deeply her spiritual anguish and the inner world she hid from her caregivers. To me it was a marvel that she had persisted in her quest to find God, to find evidence of His presence in her life. To the end, she didn't want her life to have been in vain.

For her the question was not what diagnosis she carried but where God was: *Does God come to the seclusion room?* This was the title of an article she wrote as she searched for answers. In her poetry, her articles, her journals, and her reading, this was the question she struggled to answer: How can one know the presence of God, the Spirit, when one's inner world is so tormented? Was she a devil? Was she evil? Was her mental illness a sign of God's punishment? Was there hope for someone like her? What is the meaning of suffering?

It is challenging enough to attempt an answer to these questions when one is considered "sane," but when suffering from "insanity," it is like climbing Mount Everest on crutches. How do you know? What do you know? And if you have a mental illness, to whom can you ask your questions without being given more medication and being called delusional or hyperreligious?

Beverly had not been raised in a religious family. She was an agnostic until her first year of college, when she started going to an Episcopal student center, where she found tolerance rather than condemnation for her doubts about God. Gradually, in this atmosphere she began to believe in God and was baptized and confirmed, but none of this freed her from her sense of guilt. From the time of her baptism, except for some recurrent periods of agnosticism, she attended church whether she was in the hospital or out.

The struggles between doubt and belief and between God's goodness and her sense of evil were the dominant themes of Beverly's inner journey, one she traveled alone because she could not risk revealing it to psychiatric ears. Her caregivers referred pejoratively to "Beverly's devil thing" and never explored what it meant.

Often men and women who were sexually abused as children see themselves as evil; they feel that somehow *they* did this terrible thing, and they view their anguish as punishment from God—a divine judgment. In a journal entry, Beverly does mention one positive encounter with an elderly Catholic priest who visited her during one of her hospital stays. His gentleness and acceptance allowed her to consider that perhaps God could be gentle with her, too.

After meeting this priest, she noted that she wanted to lean more on God and far less on capricious, inconsistent, and often callous psychiatric personnel. She remarked, "In drawing closer to Him, though it didn't heal me, I gained increased strength to endure. I knew He was there for me, despite His painful silences."

In a later entry she continues: "Over and over again, in moments of extreme darkness and despair, I had a sense that God was there for me, sometimes turning my agony into joy—this enabled me to continue on with the struggle and terror. I have read a great many books on God and suffering and extracted hopeful and comforting messages, compiling my own 'Pain Book.' Only at one point did the silence, coupled with despair, seem truly more that I could bear, and I took an overdose."

Here was a woman engaged in two battles: one to receive care and be accepted and loved and the other for her soul. With amazing tenacity, she persevered on both fronts. Her caregivers responded only to her aberrant and extremely off-putting behavior. She was mentally ill; that was the beginning and the end of their vision.

Dismissed as "religiously preoccupied" and into her "devil thing," she was scorned, carrying not a red letter *A* on her chest but the dreaded *B* for "borderline" on her chart—one of her many diagnoses.[2] No one ever seemed to ask about her life outside the clinic, what she did when she wasn't in the ER driving people crazy. If the providers had asked, they would have encountered a different person.

Without help, she wasn't able to bring the different elements of her life together. She was like someone standing in the ocean in the midst of a ferocious storm, tossed about in the sea of her own emotions. The depression, the terror, the pain, the anxiety had such force that she could not, at those times, access her own strength, her own religious convictions. Her writing was her attempt to keep herself as "together" as she could and to attend to where she sensed God was in her life. In a meticulous way, on a daily basis, save for those times when she was too over-whelmed, Bev recorded her feelings of guilt, joy, depression, pain, and goodness, as well as her daily activities and self-care. It is in these reflections that her struggle is most poignantly realized:

> *A Philosophy for my life, especially if I am in pain (written in pain):*
> When you are in pain, you must 1) wait for the relief
> which has always come by God's grace; 2) function as well as
> you can with as little self-pity and self-hatred as possible; 3) still
> "be kind to all I meet" as much as I can; 4) take it one day at a
> time; 5) treat yourself and others as lovingly as possible. When
> you have failed, accept God's, others', and your own forgiveness
> as soon as possible. Then with His help, "Take up your bed
> and walk."

In the emotionally safe holding environment created by Janet the psychology intern, Beverly gradually began to reveal not only the painful aspects of her inner life but also her spiritual quest. With Janet she shared her journal entries, articles, draw-ings, poetry, and the literature she was reading, as well as her doubts and her faith. By seeing herself in the mirror of Janet's acceptance, Beverly began to form a different image of herself and made fewer visits to the ER. She stopped cutting herself and had shorter, more infrequent stays in the hospital. There were no more suicide attempts.

How is it that her spiritual convictions didn't prevent her from being such a burden to those who treated her before Janet did? If her spiritual life was so central, why didn't it make more of a difference in her life? Was she deluded about it?

For Beverly, her faith never took away her pain. In the grip of a severe depression or extreme anxiety, she didn't feel that her faith made a difference. She had a crushing sense of being in a darkness that she could not shake, no matter how hard she tried. Her bent posture suggested that for years she had carried a weight that made doing the smallest things such a struggle, yet she did her calculus, knitted socks, studied French, wrote poetry, had articles published—and hoped.

Intellectually, Bev knew that kindness, beauty, and caring were often there, but they weren't reaching her. She couldn't grasp the life rafts being thrown her way. Ironically, it was after being diagnosed with cancer that she was able to let herself be touched by and receive the care of others; she no longer felt evil.

In an article titled "Spiritual Issues of the Mentally Ill," Beverly wrote:

> Spiritually I am quite the novice, just beginning to learn of Him—there are still within me great doubts, pride, sin, narcissism, terror, and pain. But there are ideas and experiences I have encountered along the way that I would like to share. If I share my "lessons" with you and you share your "lessons" with me, not only are we offering gracious gifts to one another in our common struggle with pain and illness, but perhaps we can increasingly feel our journey a less lonely one, and join hands as we face together both our adversities and our hopes.

Beverly wanted to teach, to call people to awareness. It is evident in her writings that she never used her faith to deny her illness or her pain, recognizing that her own journey, like that of many others, had been filled with paradoxes, doubts, and seemingly unanswerable questions. Because of her own suffering, she identified with the poor and the vulnerable: "Despite the incredible amount of suffering I experience and see others experiencing, I have real hope—and that hope has given me comfort in my darkest hours."

I found it amazing that her spirit had not been totally defeated, given her history.

For her, courage was not about heroic deeds, loudly applauded by others, but the quieter hour-by-hour, even minute-by-minute decisions on how to deal with adversity—anxiety, depression, voices, or any problem that plagued her. With her small library, her Pain Book filled with hopeful quotes, her intellectual pursuits, and her journals, she exercised that courage.

For me, her life illustrates two salient lessons. First, by attending only to her mental illness, her caregivers treated only half the person she was. Ignoring the potential strength of faith, they unwittingly prolonged her distress and theirs. Second, faith—that is, a commitment to someone or something bigger than yourself—is a compass that keeps you pointing in the right direction when all else seems lost. Beverly found meaning in prayer, in participation in a faith community, in writing, and in her intellectual pursuits. She waited, and she kept going, like T. S. Eliot, who wrote:

> *I said to my soul, be still and wait without hope*
> *For hope would be hope for the wrong thing; wait without love*
> *For love would be love of the wrong thing; there is yet faith*
> *But the faith and the love and the hope are all in the waiting.*
> *Wait without thought, for you are not ready for thought.*
> *So the darkness shall be the light and the stillness, the dancing.*[3]

Surrounded by love and compassion, Beverly's waiting was rewarded. In the end, she received what she had sought.

3

Creative Spirits

Consultations to an ongoing therapy are always instructive for me because I learn as much about the therapist as I do about the client and myself. On one occasion I was asked to meet with an art therapist who presented me with a client's drawing: "I am concerned that Mark is becoming psychotic. He has drawn this picture of the world with a large bird over it. And he says he is expressing hope in it." As I looked at it, I recalled the words of Genesis 1:2, "Now the earth was a formless void, there was darkness over the deep, and God's spirit hovered over the water," along with those of Gerard Manley Hopkins:

> And though the last lights off the black West went
> Oh, morning, at the brown brink eastward, springs—
> Because the Holy Ghost over the bent
> World broods with warm breast and with ah! bright wings.[1]

Hopkins, a Jesuit priest who suffered with depression, was expressing his own hope-filled belief in the presence of God's Spirit, hovering over the world. Knowing and loving both Scripture and poetry, I looked at the client's work through a different lens.

I mentioned the biblical reference and the poem to the art therapist and explained that perhaps the client was expressing hope and the sense that God had not abandoned him. Rather than exploring what she deemed "psychotic," I invited her to ask him about the image and what it suggested instead of automatically interpreting it as a manifestation of his illness. I suggested that she try to find a way to focus on his strengths while not ignoring his depression by exploring the image as a possible expression of his healthier spirit. If "beauty is in the eye of the beholder," as the saying goes, then is illness also? (Here I am using "healthier spirit" to refer to the aspect of a person that is the source of energy, courage, resilience, and hope that enables the person to connect with self and others.)

Because of their illness, the clients see themselves as wounded spirits, damaged goods, for the most part neither religious nor spiritual. The constant struggle with their symptoms, feelings of rage, bitterness, resentment, and regret leads to a sense of self-hatred. For many, symptoms of their illness make attending a house of worship difficult. Though they may talk to God, they don't think this is praying because they aren't using scripted words.

The benchmarks for the ways most people define themselves as religious or spiritual are missing from their lives. As noted in Chapter Two, Beverly had her own benchmarks, but no one noticed. When I started the groups, I, too, had a limited view of what it meant to be religious or spiritual. I wasn't considering poetry, art, or music as subjects for the Spiritual Beliefs and Values groups. I was still conflating *spiritual* with *religious*.

Before the reforms of Vatican II, when I wore the nun's habit, my headpiece was a starched coif that prevented me from seeing to the side; I could only see directly in front of me. This has become my symbol of how my ideas about what it means to be religious or spiritual were equally constricted.

Three clients in particular have challenged me to reflect on the power of the arts to engage the spirit, thereby expanding my notion of what it means to be religious or spiritual. You may well say that the arts have always been a significant part of the world's great religious traditions. But for me, it was something new to consider how art, poetry, or music expressed and nurtured the spirit, especially the wounded spirit, in a way that wasn't overtly tied to traditional ritual or observance.

Jennifer is a tall woman with an aristocratic bearing, impos-
ing in many ways—articulate, creative, and intelligent. Her strong
physical presence belies the anxious, fearful person who has lived
inside for so many years. The enormous difference between her
external and internal reality has been a source of pain most of
her life.

Unlike many others in the day treatment program, Jennifer's
family enjoyed material prosperity, summers in Maine, travel, and
educational opportunities, but it was also burdened by a history
of mental illness. The family attended the Episcopal church, but
the harsh and demanding sermons Jennifer heard offered her no
sense of a loving, compassionate God. She blamed herself for the
chaos in her family and experienced her mother's anger and frus-
tration as a sign that God was also angry with her.

In church she experienced dread, but outside the hallowed
walls she learned about the mystery and majesty of nature from
a doctor who was a friend of the family. Frequently, he would
take her on walks and point out to her the exquisite wildflowers,
the immensity of the galaxies, and the ways of animals. With his
comments on God's awesome creation, she learned to connect
God with beauty and life, not with demands and expectations.
She found comfort and solace in nature, yet for the most part her
life was filled with confusion, fear, and depression. For years she
masked her pain until she could no longer bear it. In her twenties
she was hospitalized.

Like others in this book, Jennifer has spent her adult life
in the mental health system. During one of her hospital stays,
she heard the damning words of a doctor—that she would never
overcome her illness, that the incredible, overpowering hell of a
mental hospital was to be her perpetual fate.

But contrary to his prediction, with new medications, good
psychiatric care, the stability of the day treatment program, an
apartment of her own, a cat, and her art and poetry, she has

achieved, in the words of one of her poems, "Close to the mystery, some wisdom won, some fears undone."

Poignantly she expressed this: "Our true natures are bled out of us by some religious teachings, terrifying family experiences, and the pain of mental illness. We are not just pieces of damaged psyches. When you get rid of the toxic material many of us have carried from our early experiences, the majestic spirit can emerge."

To this day, I see Jennifer battle with powerful feelings that can overwhelm her; I also hear her express the pure pleasure of painting, through which she sees the universe as a hymn of endless joy and constant change. In her painting and poetry she works out the puzzle of her life. The lines of a Rilke poem come to mind:

> Let everything happen to you: beauty and terror.
> Just keep going. No feeling is final.
> Don't let yourself lose me.[2]

For me the tragedy of mental illness is the way that it can consume a life. The ability to appreciate vibrant colors, to capture images in the power of well-chosen words, to find hope in a sunrise, is almost destroyed. It is people like Jennifer who make me wonder what would happen if we were to refocus our mental health treatment on the creative—not only as art therapy or as a way of understanding or giving expression to anguish but also as a way of celebrating what is alive, strong, resilient, and spiritual.

I had entered religious life in the 1950s, when the formation was modeled on the monastic tradition. The emphasis was on creating a controlled environment aimed at fostering a person's spiritual life. To this end, the more human aspects of life were tightly regulated. Most of the women who were my companions welcomed this kind of structure, as they were intent on pursuing a relationship with God. At the time I had no idea what an inner life meant, but I dutifully obeyed all the rules and took as "Gospel truth" all I was told, thinking that in that way I might find an inner life. But in doing so, I unconsciously numbed my lively, creative, and inquisitive spirit.

As a young nun, I was told, among many other negative messages received, that I was not artistic, although in my family I had been considered quite a creative spirit. During a school vacation one year, we were invited to do something creative, a rare event in the overly structured and rigid environment of religious life then. At the time I was having a great deal of difficulty. After three and a half years of formation in our novitiate, I had become anxious, scrupulous, depressed, and generally miserable. I was a failure as a teacher, was disliked in the community because of my rigidity and anxiety, and had no sense of God in my life. I felt neither religious nor spiritual.

That afternoon I went off by myself and sculpted the wounded hand of Jesus. I had never done any work with clay and am not sure why I chose this, other than the fact that I could use my own hand as a model. In retrospect, I see it as an expression of some of the pain I felt at the time. Although it was years ago, I still remember the pleasure I took in this creative act.

At the end of the afternoon, each nun was to bring her piece to the community room but not to label it or identify who created it. As I listened to murmurs of admiration, I was pleased with my handiwork and with myself. The superior of the community then held up each piece of art for the rest of us to examine and asked us to guess the identity of the artist. As we went around the room, no one attached my name to the sculpted hand; in fact, I was not linked with any piece of art.

When I announced that the hand was mine, amazement and incredulity were voiced: "*You* did *that?*" I heard dismay, not admiration: Clearly, no one thought I had that kind of ability, nor was there any interest in why I had sculpted the wounded hand of Jesus.

I remember being crushed; it seemed difficult for the other nuns to look beyond my failures. Because I was doing so poorly in every area of my life, I wanted so much to be seen as having worth. Doing the sculpture had given me joy and a sense of life. At the end of the gathering, I took my sculpture, crushed it, and went back to struggling with what I thought it meant to be a "good religious," one who was obedient and self-effacing.

My experience and my work with the clients have convinced me that there is more to a person than his or her diagnosis. We need to have a curiosity about what is at the heart of a person and foster that, whether we call it spiritual or not. The bird my client drew; my sculpted hand; a painting Jennifer did after 9/11—they are all attempts to communicate some truth and a desire to be heard or seen.

Shortly after the attack on the World Trade Center, one of the group's sessions began with the members sharing their fears.

Russell said, "Whenever I hear a plane, I am afraid."

Bud responded, "I know what it is like to live with fear. Since age sixteen, I've had a major depression. I've had some good years, but then the depression comes back. I'm always afraid, even in the good times."

Jennifer said, "I'm scared that the country is going to put so much money into the military that our benefits will be cut. The mentally ill are going to suffer even more." She was so right.

Lucy, who had been Beverly's friend, asked to play a tape, *Chicken Soup for the Soul*. I was touched by her contribution, because for years demonic voices have dominated her waking hours. The story on the tape described an auctioneer trying to sell a very old, beat-up violin, but since it had no bow, it didn't attract any bidders. Finally a man came forward and bought the violin; bow in hand, he began to play beautiful music.

I asked the clients for their interpretation.

James said, "I think it was about seeing value beneath appearances."

Jennifer admitted, "I feel guilty when I want to check out, knowing that's not what God wants."

Russell hastened to respond: "You have so many wonderful gifts. Out of your pain, you bring so many gifts to the community."

"Thank you," said Jennifer. "That helps."

I asked the group, "Do you think we always let others know the values we see in them, like the violinist who saw the beauty in the beat-up violin?"

Lucy replied, "There's a song about a father and son, about how important it is to let a person know what you think while he's still here." To me that sounded like a reference to those who had died and the people who probably left home on 9/11 without telling their loved ones how precious they were to them.

Bud spoke up: "A lot of people got killed on September 11th, and I think that we ought to get the people who did it and kill them all."

Russell cautioned, "But we have to be careful not to judge all Muslims."

"Don't tell me that," Bud replied angrily. "What they did was unspeakable." He was unabashedly giving expression to the rage many felt.

Reaching into her bag, Jennifer said, "To remind myself that they are people, I painted a picture of a Muslim woman from a card I had. I don't think that God has abandoned the world but that we have abandoned God."

Executed in soft pastels, the painting showed a woman's face shrouded by a veil. She looked out with sad, tender eyes. As the members of the group looked at the painting, their silence enveloped the room.

Bud said, "But those people say they are doing this for God. What kind of thinking is that?" He was right; so much violence has been done in the name of God, in the name of religion, in defense of what is "right."

Elaine blurted out abruptly: "I can't take this conversation. I am leaving." Three other people also got up to leave but returned in a few minutes.

Just as fear gripped the nation, in a particular way fear gripped the members of the group because they knew their own fragility and their dependence on a system that doesn't always consider them. Yet with her painting, Jennifer invited us to see Muslims as human beings, to resist generalizing about "the enemy." Her portrait, an invitation to compassion, was more powerful than the sermon I heard in church the following Sunday. As the Japanese say, "One seeing is worth a thousand hearings." Her portrait was also an invitation to see Jennifer in a different light.

In the same group, drawing on his Buddhist practice, Russell invited the other members to focus on their inner selves—to look inward to find strength, ways to combat fear, anxiety, and rage.

Over and over, Russell is the one who calls me back to a grounded way of being. From him I have learned to be more comfortable with questions and to acknowledge that I don't have the answers. Having grown up in the Catholic church in the 1940s and 1950s, I learned a sense of certitude about religious truths that made it a leap for me to acknowledge "not knowing." That sense of certitude was reinforced by a religious formation that was rigorous and demanding. Questioning the system was not encouraged.

Russell is a good-looking man in his late fifties, brawny, with broad shoulders and a firm potbelly. A baseball cap with visor forward is his signature, covering his graying, reddish-brown hair. A plaid shirt, jeans, and a beat-up leather or denim jacket are his standard wear. His kind eyes, warm smile, and gentle demeanor bear witness to the fruit of his years of Zen practice but give no clue to the years of chaos he knew prior to being in the day treatment program.

Like other suburban kids, he started drinking as an adolescent so that he would be more "socially acceptable." His experience of church didn't help him when a classmate died and he had his own brush with death as he tried to save a drowning friend. Somehow in the weekly sermons, he didn't find answers to the existential questions these events triggered, and so he left the Episcopal church.

In the late 1960s, like many others, he dropped out of college, smoked pot, drank a lot, and became a "flower child" in California. As I listened to him describe these vagabond years of getting stoned, negotiating an on-again, off-again relationship with a woman whom he married, hitching across Canada on freight trains, living in hiking cabins in the mountains, and embracing Transcendental Meditation, I was struck by how incredibly different all our journeys are.

Beverly had spent most of those years cycling and recycling through the mental health system, pursuing her own inner journey. I had spent them safely enclosed in a convent, unaware of the dramatic changes afoot. Russell had spent them wandering the country. How curious that our paths crossed in this psychiatric day treatment setting!

Though Transcendental Meditation sustained Russell for a time, it didn't help him settle down. In Colorado he found his way to a Buddhist center and then went to California to help build a Tibetan Buddhist temple. There he "ran afoul" of the laypeople who were also working on the temple and ended up on the streets in Berkeley, where he started to hear voices: "They were grandiose. One time, I asked an elderly gentleman sitting on a bench waiting for the bus if he thought I was the great, powerful Tibetan

God, as the voices told me. He looked at me, bearded, unkempt, forlorn, and said, 'I don't think so.' That actually helped."

After a run-in with the police, he returned east, where he was hospitalized for depression. For Russell, the diagnosis of a mental illness was like running into a brick wall. While struggling with his illness and his unrecognized alcohol problem, he was introduced to Zen Buddhism and was allowed to move into a Zen center. He became serious about a meditation practice, got sober, joined the psychiatric day treatment program, and moved into a small condo purchased with money from his mother's estate.

Of all the spiritual paths he has trod, the Buddhist practice of sitting and chanting has been the one that changed his life:

> Buddhist teaching says, "It takes a great question, great faith, and great courage to follow a spiritual path." I see the great courage for me in dealing with all my hospitalizations and several suicide attempts. For me, the practice keeps clearing out the stuff that gets in my way, the bad karma that takes me off course. I have a real appreciation of my life these days.
>
> Chanting in my Zen practice, playing my guitar, and singing allow me to express feelings that have been quiet for a long period of time. Music gives voice to parts of me I can't express in any other way. If you talk to someone about your depression, they aren't likely to listen for too long, but if you sing the blues, they will include you in their life, and you can include them in yours. When I sing, I am in touch with my spirit.

For Russell, music is a lifeline, a way of connecting with others, of being in community, of breaking down isolation—the way some people use religion. Music and his Zen practice reinforce each other. Russell practices to stay centered and plays to stay connected, the inner and outer movement that is at the heart of all religious traditions and spiritual practices.

More than any other client, Russell has invited me to let go of categories and to pay attention to how music nourishes my spirit. My mother once told me that when she was nursing me, she listened to the opera and craved carrots. I love both opera and carrots.

Just as Russell's Buddhist approach has stretched me, so has that of Andrea, the first client to make me question the distinction between being religious and being spiritual.

Andrea joined the group in its first year when I was very focused on the religious aspects of the clients' histories. What were the religious traditions of their families? What beliefs did they hold? What religious messages had they learned? I never asked clients what nourished their spirits, and I certainly was not attentive to the varieties of ways in which my own spirit was nourished—or not. When Roberta mentioned her poetry in the first session of the group, I invited her to bring it in only as a way of affirming her as a person, not because I believed it related to the Spiritual Beliefs and Values group.

Early on, Andrea shared with the group that her grandmother had "diddled her to death about being Jewish." Because her wealthy grandmother was rigid, unaffectionate, and demanding of her servants, Andrea was turned off by religion. She made me think of how profoundly our religious histories are shaped by significant others in our lives. My own grandmother was the quintessential grandmother, a woman whose faith and love for her grandchildren were as large as her bosom. She would always say, "The Sacred Heart of Jesus will not let you down." And she knew whereof she spoke, because that faith had been her rock during my grandfather's hospitalizations for depression.

Over time Andrea began to question the difference between being spiritual and being religious, a distinction that was becoming more widespread in the 1980s as people left their religious traditions but pursued other paths, such as Eastern spiritual practices. Now it is commonplace to hear a person say, "I am spiritual but not religious."

Andrea had gone to elementary and secondary Hebrew school but did not have a bat mitzvah, probably because her parents were in the midst of a divorce. The celebration of the High Holy Days was more of an ethnic observance, not an expression of faith or of a connection to a larger sense of meaning. When I first celebrated a Seder with the clients, described in a later chapter, Andrea was awestruck at the meaning of the ceremony and its relevance for her life. The journey of the Hebrews from slavery under the Egyptians through the desert to the freedom of the Promised Land resonated with her own struggle to gain freedom from the oppression of mental illness.

Since age fourteen, when her parents divorced, she felt she had been wandering in her own desert. Her father became psychotic, and she was forced to choose between her two parents. She felt totally isolated and withdrew into herself. Because she continued to do well in school, no one seemed concerned. This lack of interest was particularly troublesome when she developed a crush on a boy in art class. Rather than helping her understand her sexuality, her mother took her out of the class.

Because her mother has always encouraged her artistic endeavors and placed great expectations on her but didn't affirm Andrea as a person, she has felt ambivalent about her art. Developing her musical and artistic gifts and regarding them as expressions of her vibrant spirit has been a challenge. She learned both in school and at home that religion was a crutch, the "opiate of the people," and a sign of weakness. Thus it has been a struggle for her to think about the possibility of a Higher Being. For several years Andrea dropped out of the group. In retrospect, I see this as her attempt to separate herself from any religious or spiritual influence. At the time she told us that psychology was her religion.

About two years ago she asked if she could rejoin the group because she was in a different place. For years Andrea has struggled to separate herself from her mother and become more of her own person, recognizing and accepting both her uniqueness and her ordinariness. When she rejoined the group, she said she felt she was freer to acknowledge that there are many paths to enlightenment and that each of us makes our own path, which means following our heart.

I saw a real difference in her; but it wasn't until I interviewed Andrea about the role her art and music play in getting her in touch with her spirit that I felt I had touched her core. Even when she was in the hospital, "psychotic as all hell," as she described it, she learned to crochet. Even when most burdened by her illness, she did her art, working in black and white; using colors stirred up too many feelings.

"I have decided there is some kind of meaning in the world," she told me. "For me, my meaning is my art, my music. It gets me away from my illness, of a sense of being disabled. Theater allows us to look at realities through the mind's eye of another. The arts allow us to have mirrors on ourselves and make us more human, more connected."

As I sat with her, I was in awe of how far she had come on her journey, and I regretted that my constricted vision had blinded me to the fact that her creativity was a place of light and life for her. I wondered what would have happened if the superior of the community had recognized some talent in me when I did the hand of Jesus or had at least explored its significance. Might I have become an artist rather than a psychologist?

Jennifer, Russell, and Andrea have expanded my vision about what it means to be spiritual and have also affected the ways in which I work with all the clients. Since the three are all members of the morning group, one day I asked the members of the afternoon group to recall an experience that gave them a sense of life, of creative energy, of connection with what is most essential.

As we went around the room, both their responses and their reflections touched me. Some were drawing on recent experiences and others from distant memories.

Though their comments may sound like Hallmark cards, the men and women expressing them were living in anything but a picture-perfect world. For them, daily living is like attempting a marathon. Every step in a day requires a lot of energy:

"I wake early, cross the street, buy some coffee at Au Bon Pain, and watch the sun rise. For me, that is a hopeful way of beginning the day."

"Once I went out to Gay Head on Martha's Vineyard. The highly colored cliffs with their various hues of reds, browns, and oranges contrasted sharply with the green and blue ocean. As the sun reflected off the water, it created a breathtaking panorama."

"I love my room. I have a bed, a dresser, a mantel with pictures of my family, and my few precious things. My room is a place of peace."

"From the porch of my mother's house in Vermont, I can see the Green Mountains. At dusk, the pinks, the oranges, the purples on the trees transform the mountains."

"When we were little, we would go to my grandmother's house. On the way there we went down a road where the trees formed a canopy over the road. It was lovely and so calming."

"I thought about the mosque in Turkey. The oriental prayer rugs were a red pattern, and the interior was marble. I still remember the sense of peace there."

Each person had painted a picture I could see and enjoy. When the group ended, I knew, sadly, that in the course of the week, their anxiety, depression, anger, concerns about medication, and fears of losing benefits and for some even housing would loom so large on the horizon that they would lose touch with the life-giving memories and experiences they had just described. I was fairly certain that they would not talk about this part of their lives in any other group or in individual work with their therapists, where they focus on abusive families, their medications, suicidal thoughts, symptom management, and addictions.

What struck me forcefully was that in recalling their experiences, they were in touch with a part of themselves that was intensely tuned in to life at those moments. As we ended the group, one client said, "This group on Monday is like going to church on Sunday; we are reminded that we are more than our illness." That I happened to agree with him made me reflect on the benefits of attending a religious service. Though there are many reasons to participate in religious rituals, chief among them is a connection with the sacred, with something "other," perhaps greater, in the context of a community. For me both were present that day. I felt sad and glad: sad that the flicker of life I saw would be so quickly quenched by the reality of their week and glad that at least for a moment they were in touch with an experience that was life-affirming.

In listening to and observing Jennifer, Russell, and Andrea and the other clients, I have reflected on the role of creativity in my own life, where I am in touch with the Creator, where my spirit is nourished, when and where I feel most alive, most connected to others. It is not only in the confines of a church, at a religious ceremony, or when I am praying. It is reading poetry at breakfast, listening to a violin concerto, taking photos; it is in the pounding of the waves on seashore and in preparing a lovely dinner for friends.

The art therapist, working with her client, was only able to see psychosis in his drawing. When I was constricted by my religious formation, I only inquired about a person's religious history. Educated by my clients, I have expanded my notion of what it means to be religious, to be spiritual. The source of the word *religion*, the Latin *religio*, is "to bind back." Religion is meant to bind us back to the Creator, not to bind us internally with knots of fear, anxiety, and prejudice. *Spiritual*, with its root in spirit or breath, refers to the source of life.

With these men and women I have reclaimed my creative spirit as I have helped them reaffirm their own. Together we have been reconnected to what is essential.

4

Buddy, an Unlikely Prophet

uddy was not a creative spirit, nor had he assiduously pursued a spiritual journey as Beverly had. To my knowledge, the two never even met. But coincidentally, they died in the same hospice house, both succumbing to cancer after fighting valiantly against their mental illness. Unlike Beverly, Bud, as his friends called him, had not alienated his caregivers over the years. He had endeared himself to all who knew him, determined not to alienate others with the effects of his illness. For me, that determination was part of the mystery of who he was.

When I first met him at the day treatment center, Bud had suffered for more than thirty years with major depression, including manic episodes. When he was a child he attended the Catholic grammar school that later housed the psychiatric day treatment program. Life takes odd twists and turns.

Bud joined the program in 1996 and was a steadfast member until January 6, 2003, the day he died. He was fifty-seven. When I noted his short, square, muscular build, I was reminded of his Irish roots and of people working the land. A drooping eyelid gave his face a sad look: he would have been typecast perfectly in a James Cagney movie.

Honest, intelligent, feisty, sometimes opinionated but always kind, a true gentleman, Buddy was a central figure in the day treatment program and for seven years a key member of the Spiritual Beliefs and Values group. He left his mark on everyone in the program. Fenced in by poverty, a lack of education, and mental illness, he lived his entire life in a circumscribed area in Boston, yet his mind went far beyond the few blocks of the housing project. In one of our conversations he said, "Nancy, you know, I just love to learn. That is why I like your group; I enjoy having my mind stretched by others' beliefs."

Bud loved to question and to challenge people, especially me. He reflected on theological questions that I had just accepted, such as the thirty lost years of Jesus' life. To him it made no sense that if God were going to spend time on this earth, He would have done so in prolonged obscurity. Though I never asked Bud, I wondered if he said this because so much of his life had seemed like a waste as well.

Faithfully he attended my group for seven years, first as a quiet but intense listener and observer and then as one of the most thoughtful and active participants. Reflecting on the coincidence of having been in grammar school and in a psychiatric program in the same building, Bud recalled an incident with one of his teachers:

> When we were in grammar school in this building and went to
> the church next door, the nuns would count heads to make sure
> we were all present. They wanted us all to excel and to do well
> in the world. One day when I was acting up, Sister Mary, or
> "Old Ironsides," as we called her, told me to go to the cloakroom,
> where she said, "Put water under your eyes, messy up." Then she
> made noises, pretending she was hitting me.
>   She put it in my head that Jesus would never leave me.
> I used to visit her until she died.

I suspected that he kept these visits to himself.

As he silently sat in the group week after week, I think he was evaluating me, deciding whether he would trust me and the other participants. Men and women who have spent years in the mental health system have learned not to trust too readily. Providers have to earn that precious commodity.

Finally one day Bud revealed that he'd spent much of his life angry with God. For him the combination of mental illness and poverty seemed too much. With fists raised, he described looking up at God, cursing and swearing at Him. The man reminded me of the prophet Jeremiah, who felt it would have been better not to have been born. Examining his fate and those of his closest companions, with an expression of intense desperation, Bud asked, *"What kind of God would give someone a life like this?"*

I had no response. Instinctively, I knew that Buddy would reject any cliché or pat religious response. I had to answer him from my heart, as he was speaking from his. His integrity demanded my honesty, and all I had was my silent acceptance of his question. Over and over, through the years, his questions challenged me, inviting me to examine what I truly thought and believed.

More than once, as we concluded the group, he approached me to ask if I was upset with him for being angry with God. For Bud, I was "God's businesswoman," and he was anxious about being mad at my Boss. I assured him that it was not just OK but understandable. To his relief, I resisted defending God.

One day he told us that over the past several months, he'd been feeling so paranoid that he couldn't leave his apartment. In desperation, he asked Jesus for help, and after a few minutes, he became calmer, went out, and bought some groceries. From then on, he knelt down every morning and evening, asked for help, and then thanked God for the day.

When Bud was able to speak of his anger in the group, it lessened a bit, but when he was diagnosed with cancer for the second and third time, his rage returned. He said he had given up on God. Once when I commented that his fury suggested that he still had a relationship with God, similar to that of the Jewish prophets who often cried out to God in their anger, he said, "Nancy, don't try to get me to talk to Him. I don't want to have anything more to do with Him." I felt the intensity of his rage; I loved his honesty but was sad that he didn't perceive the connection with God I thought he had.

He was taking responsibility for his anger, for the faith that enabled him to turn to God for help, and then for the sense of betrayal that made him turn his face away from God. Before God and others, he was so clearly and unashamedly who he was.

In July 2002, when Bud told the group of his third diagnosis of cancer, he knew his days were limited. This was a wake-up call for me. After inheriting Beverly's journals, I had been toying with the idea of writing a book. Daunted by the task, I felt that my commitment was feeble. When I heard his prognosis, I was suddenly mobilized: there was no time for procrastination. I began to interview Buddy.

I told him I envisaged a book about spirituality and mental illness and the resilient men and women I had met at the day treatment programs. He was thrilled to be part of the story. Unexpectedly, his life had new meaning. Though I never had the opportunity to tell him, he had deeply affected me, more than I recognized at that time.

Quietly, but with obvious enthusiasm, he responded, "I've had people in my life who told me that someone should write about me—smart people, people I sat down to eat with, went to lectures with, even some Harvard types. They accepted me and liked the way I put things across." What he wanted readers to know was that in their own neighborhood there are people with mental illness who were asking for God. Astutely, he remarked that the medical world does not have all the answers: "People with mental illness have healthy spirits. We may be crazy, but we are not stupid."

This classic Buddy statement separates craziness from intelligence, a distinction the general public often fails to make.

Starting that summer, we met weekly at the day treatment program in a room with a pool table, a fitting place to speak with someone who could play a mean game. When his failing health prevented him from attending the program, we met in his apartment.

I came with my agenda. I wanted to know about Buddy's soul, about how he came to be the person he was, given all that he'd suffered. But he wanted to tell me his story instead of dealing with my God questions. I learned to listen and take my lead from him. He taught me to look at life as a whole and that the "God question" could be answered in the way one lives. As with all good teachers, his lessons went far beyond the classroom.

Buddy was born into a family whose circumstances undermined rather than abetted his natural intelligence. Buddy was one of nine brothers and sisters, and the family lived in a five-room apartment in a housing project. Growing up, he took more than his share of life's beatings, literally and figuratively. His father worked for the city "on the orange trucks," the description Bud used to avoid using the words *garbage collector*. An innately proud man, he hated the fact that his small apartment was furnished with what his Dad picked up off the streets. In his twenties, Bud bought his mother the only living room set she ever had.

The family's poverty, exacerbated by his father's drinking, determined more than the interior décor, or the lack of it. Without money for the bus or for lunch, he walked to school and frequently went hungry. Paper in his shoes covered the holes and kept out the water, a daily reminder of the family's meager resources. Because he endeared himself to people, on school days when the principal was absent, the person behind the lunch counter gave him a free meal.

Bud knew depravation, but he was also resourceful. He and his friends did a lot of stealing. Long before guards were posted at every doorway on a college campus, they went to nearby colleges to grab wallets. While his father was earning only $65 a week for a family of nine kids, Buddy was bringing home $80 to $90 a week. With some of this money, he bought his sister clothes for high school so she'd look like the other kids.

With tears in his eyes, he said, "She never forgot what I did for her, and I don't feel one bit guilty."

Given my religious upbringing, at one point in my life I knew I would have reacted to his stealing in a moralistic and judgmental way, but now I couldn't. As I noted his tears, I reflected on the reasons his family had stood by him during all the years of his depression.

When group members from families with money and education talked about their mental illness, Bud always stated in a fiery way that poverty, insecurity, and a lack of education made mental illness that much harder to bear. Not until I heard him talk about his early years did I understand his intensity. He detested poverty and the way it had shaped his life. To the day he died, he also regretted his lack of education.

In October 1963, at age sixteen, a month before John Kennedy's assassination, Buddy fell into the black hole of depression. After seeing one kid knife another at school, he went home and cried all day. The next day he refused to return to school and finally quit altogether after months of absence. More than once he thought of hanging himself but was too poor to buy the rope. As he spoke, I tried to imagine his situation, wondering where his parents were at the time.

By contrast, my mother always knew when I was under the weather and wanted to know the reason. No feigned illness or lame excuse kept me or either of my two brothers home from school. Light filled our apartment. In Bud's house, though they lived very close to one another, disconnection and darkness seemed to prevail. Days, weeks, and months spent in his apartment were broken up only by trips across the street to the settlement house, a place where the kids in the neighborhood congregated at night, safely off the streets. A volunteer social worker at the settlement house noticed his depression and took action.

To get some treatment mandated, she took him to a judge. At seventeen he was hospitalized. From the city hospital he was taken to a psychiatric hospital, where he spent the next three and a half months in pajamas in the quiet room—an adolescent male cooped up in a mental hospital. That was enough to drive a person crazy. Twice he managed to escape but was brought back by his mother and cousin. Finally he got out in 1964.

On the streets, having a mental illness was worse than having a prison record. The kids called him "the crazy one" and "Mousey." Though Bud had a talent with words, he knew that the only way he could regain power was by fighting. Despite his small stature, he was able to hold his own.

With volunteers at the settlement house, he held his ground with his intelligence. Recognizing his abilities, one of the volunteers obtained a scholarship for him at a prep school in downtown Boston. At nineteen he was moved from the freshman class to the junior class in short order. Thanks to his verbal prowess, he was put on the debate team. During the school lunch breaks, he went to the Boston Public Library and read all the international newspapers published in English. His second and last attempt at formal education was interrupted by another severe bout of depression. It seemed to come out of the blue: "One day walking to the bus stop, I knew I was getting depressed again. It would come on me just like that. In those days, people didn't understand depression. I dropped out of school."

As I listened to Bud, I thought about my own experience. Six months after my mother's death I became seriously depressed. I too felt as though I had turned a corner and stepped over an unseen ledge. For months all the things that normally brought me pleasure left me unmoved. I felt a crushing sense of being in a darkness from which I could not escape, no matter how hard I tried. Nothing, not even faith, felt like it made a difference.

After seeing a psychiatrist and taking an antidepressant, I began, slowly, to feel better. My depression was not chronic but situational. I was fortunate. But this brief encounter with the demon of depression gave me a better understanding of what men and women like Bud face in their daily, weekly, yearly battles with this illness.

In the hope of persuading his parents to send Bud back to the prep school, some of his teachers came to his house. Bud, ashamed of his father's drinking, met the visitors alone in the hallway. Though they urged him to come back, he couldn't. Shortly after he dropped out of school, one of his brothers was killed in Vietnam. Weighed down by life's pressures, both parents began to drink heavily.

For the rest of Bud's life, an unpredictable and uncontrollable depression would come in, take over, and then finally disappear at some random point—always leaving him with the fear that it would return.

Poverty, alcoholism, mental illness, and death, all before he turned twenty. As Bud told me his story, he expressed anger, sadness, and regret but never self-pity. Nor did he want that from others. To him, pity was demeaning. Bud elicited respect, affection, and admiration from everyone who knew him. He contained his own suffering and never took it out on others.

When he was in his twenties, Bud took acid with some friends and went to the roof of his building intending to jump off, but he couldn't do it. He noted wryly, "I have wanted to kill myself so many times, and now I know I am dying, and I want to hold on. I want to hold on now for my family, for the people here. I've had a hard time in life. I don't want to see others go through what I've gone through. I hate the fact that I can't do more for others."

While Bud spoke passionately about the deprivation he had known, he also talked about the numerous ways he had experienced human kindness and seemingly divine intervention. He remembered the woman who owned the convenience store where he worked as a teenager, who made him cheeseburgers when he had nothing to eat. For his brother's funeral, she bought him a suit to wear. On rainy days, when he sold newspapers, a young shop owner allowed him to stand inside his store. The janitor in his housing project used his political clout to find funding for his second term in prep school. Then there was George, the mailman, who put the extra stamps on letters to Vietnam when his family couldn't afford them. Bud noticed and was grateful for the smallest things.

He would have been surprised to know how much I thought about him after we talked, how his gratitude touched me deeply and humbled me, as I recognized how much I take for granted. His values and his valor challenged me and invited me to look at my life with new eyes, to recognize the gift in small human encounters.

During one of the last Spiritual Beliefs and Values groups he attended, the other members were despondent. Predicted financial cuts in Medicaid, the threats of terrorism, the reports of suicide bombings in Israel, the sex abuse crisis in the Catholic church—it all weighed them down. Bud, dying with cancer, rallied them with his view of God: "I don't think God wants the world to end. With all that He has created, He wants us to go forward. We are at the age where God hasn't left us. He is just making us more responsible for our actions."

Though the cancer and the medication were affecting him, and he recognized that his mind and memory were slowing down, he was still the keen observer who took great joy in seeing a group of toddlers walking along the street with their day care workers. To keep the children connected and safe, each child holds tightly onto a rope. His parting words to the group one day were words of life: "I think God gives us little children to make us feel good. A lot of people take such scenes for granted. I think it's a reward

God has given me; I notice." Each time I see a group of small children walking in a line, I think of Bud and am grateful for his vision. And I have wondered if Bud felt in some way that he too had been clinging onto a rope most of his life.

In the last two months of his life, when he was too ill to come to the program, I met with him in his apartment on the eighteenth floor of a subsidized housing complex, where he enjoyed a view of Boston. His simple place captured what was important in his life: pictures of his brothers and sisters, nieces and nephews; copies of *Sports Illustrated*; sports pennants; scratch tickets on the table; and his favorite Dunkin Donuts coffee mugs.

One day I had holiness on my mind, because I really believed Bud was holy. In his matter-of-fact way, he informed me that he never discussed "this stuff." For him, holiness was about being helpful. He cited two examples. A man in the projects had broken his leg, and a neighbor who didn't have much brought over a box of canned goods for him and his family. In Bud's mind, that made her act holy.

He also described his therapist as a knowledgeable, concerned, compassionate, and cheerful woman. Though she called herself an agnostic, to him she was holy. Bud disdained churchgoers who lack sympathy or compassion for others. To his mind, they neither practiced their religion nor were holy. Just as Jesus did, Bud railed against hypocrites. What mattered to him was the way you lived your life, not the way you talked about it.

When I remarked that sometimes he sounded like the Dalai Lama, who says his religion is kindness, Bud smiled: "Don't be going and making any saint out of me, Nancy."

One day I asked what made him tick. What made him the remarkable person he was in the face of so much adversity? Though he eschewed the idea of being remarkable, he admitted to two things in his life that made a difference: his niece Annette and some kind of religious experience.

For him, Annette was a gift from God, someone who helped him through life. Since her father wasn't around, he became like a father to her. From the time she was a baby, Bud took care of her every Friday night, except for the times he was in the hospital. At first he took care of her at his mother's apartment. When he moved to his own place after his mother's death, he brought her with him. During the week, he saved up so they could have a feast on Friday. As she got older, they'd watch videos. His world turned on her. In the throes of some of his darkest moments, when he considered suicide, it was her presence that kept him going.

With courage and straightforwardness, he described to me a recent evening in which he'd told her he was going to die: "We both started crying; she's nineteen. That was the hardest conversation I ever had with her. I talked to her about drugs and told her that you lose your motivation with marijuana—that if you're going to go to college, you need your head. She's the most important thing in my life. I have some money that I saved for her when I quit smoking. All I want for her is happiness."

I swallowed hard and looked out over the city of Boston. Here was a man who struggled to stay alive, who struggled to get out of bed on many mornings, who had been deprived of so much, yet he was totally present to his niece, the fulcrum of his life. As Saint John of the Cross said, "In the evening of life, it is only love that counts."

Here was that truth in front of me: Bud got it right.

Though Bud seldom asked to speak with me outside group meetings, on one occasion a couple of years before he knew he had terminal cancer, he wanted me to know he had a sense that he and a few other people had been singled out by God. This was his secret, and he trusted me not to share it with anyone at that time. (Subsequently he gave me permission to do so.) In our conversations before his death, I asked him more about it.

In a very lucid way, he described a manic episode when he felt a particular intimacy with God as the Source of all energy. Though he recognized that the experience occurred in the context of his illness, he also remembered the experience as something separate. He was convinced he had touched, or been touched by, something greater than himself that gave his life meaning. "I realize it is not acceptable," he told me. "People don't think of this as reality; it's my reality."

I was reluctant to judge his experience. To me it was obvious that he lived in a way that transcended the debilitating effects of his illness. Bud called to mind Carl Jung's saying, "Called or uncalled, God is present." Whether other people believed in it or not, it seemed evident that Bud was in touch with some Higher Power, some Source of Energy, a Spirit. He was generous in the face of deprivation; he was compassionate in the midst of pain and despair; he consistently sought knowledge while he battled with darkness; he stated the truth of who he was no matter who the audience was; weighed down by his own depression, he never imposed his burden on others.

With his physical energy waning, Bud directed the little he had toward ensuring that his final weeks and death would not be an encumbrance on his family. Anxiously, he waited to learn if his insurance would allow him to be accepted in a hospice house. Although he was very weak, one day he said vehemently, "This is wrong for a person to have to end his life this way—maybe to die alone because he doesn't have enough insurance to get into a hospice place. I only have a few weeks to live, and I don't want to burden others with debt. I got the cheapest burial I could, and have saved four thousand dollars for it."

Personally I felt helpless, but I also knew that the staff at the day treatment program were using all their connections to place him in the hospice program.

The week before Thanksgiving, looking like an old man, Bud returned to my group for the last time. His muscular build had given way to the ravages of the disease.

I welcomed him back from the hospital: "We are so glad you are here today, Bud." All the group members nodded their agreement. "I want to make this a good group for you."

"We'll make it a good group for all of us," he said graciously.

Jennifer told the group, "I have been feeling very paranoid for weeks, but I woke up this morning, and it was a kind of a miracle. I wasn't feeling paranoid, and I thought of you, Nancy, and decided I'd pray for you. You must carry a lot of burdens, and you need our prayers."

Jennifer was one of Bud's good friends in the program. I think she focused on me to take the pressure off him.

Bud asked, "What does it do for you, Nancy, when you hear Jennifer say that she'll pray for you?"

"It touches me deeply." It did, because I knew she meant it.

Bud said, "My brother Kevin, the priest, ends his phone conversations with 'God bless.'"

Elaine joined in: "I have a relative who says 'God bless,' and I really like that. It makes me feel closer to God."

Elaine dresses with style and wears her beautiful dark hair in a bun, usually clasped with an eye-catching comb. Speaking with an accent in a rat-a-tat-tat cadence, she can sometimes be difficult to understand.

Russell asked Bud, "What take does your brother the priest have on your illness?"

"We never do that kind of talking," Bud admitted. "He's just my brother. I grew up in the projects just like he did. When we're together, we just talk about family things. He made the choices he did for his life, and I made the choices I did."

"Russell," I asked, "what did you mean when you asked Bud what his brother's take on the illness was?"

Bud answered instead. "He knows I am dying. This is not about being cured. God's not going to hit a homer to left field for me. The medical world is doing what it can for me. I don't expect miracles. I'm not saying I don't believe in miracles, but I'm not counting on that for me."

Jennifer said, "Bud, you know we are all in mourning for you. You are so important to us, and we are really grieving for you."

Elaine agreed: "That's right—you are always so kind to me and us here."

Bud replied, "People say I am courageous, strong. I'm just doing what I have to do, and I'm doing it the only way I know how to do it."

"Well, you're doing a damn good job," Russell said.

Russell echoed my sentiments. Bud was doing a damn good job of living and dying, right up to the end.

Jennifer continued speaking: "You have meant so much to everyone in the community—we are going to miss you terribly. Your dying makes me think about my mother. When I was just a little girl, maybe three or four, my mother took my brother and me to the cemetery and pointed to a spot and said, 'David, this place is for you.' And then she looked at me and said, 'Jennifer, there is no place for you.'" Tears came to her eyes.

"That's just horrible," said James, and everyone in the group nodded in agreement. Though James has also struggled with physical difficulties, he doesn't feel sorry for himself. He is always the first to empathize with someone else's pain.

"I have a pain in my heart," Pat said. "I think I need to leave the group." I think everyone had heart pain, but only Pat named it.

Jennifer continued, "That's why I don't want to be with my mother for Thanksgiving. I am wondering if I should go to the Cape."

Elaine broke in: "Jennifer, I was counting on you being here; that's why I decided I wasn't going to be with my family. You said you would be here. It's not good for you to be with your family. We're your family. I feel like you're betraying me."

"Elaine," Jennifer retorted, "don't lay that on me. Don't make your decisions based on what I do." I knew that some of this anger wasn't about the two of them but everyone's anger that Bud was dying.

"My mother is in her eighties," Jennifer said. "Maybe this will be her last Thanksgiving. Elaine, it's not about you."

Elaine got up and left, saying, "I don't like this conflict." But she didn't stay away long. When she returned, she addressed Jennifer calmly. "I am sorry that I said that. You are right; you have to do what you have to do. But I just wanted you to know that I'll miss you if you are not here."

As he sat silently, I wondered if Bud was thinking that this was about him. I spoke up: "Elaine, I am glad you were able to come back and apologize to Jennifer."

"We love each other, but we can push each other's buttons," she admitted.

"I think that is true," I said. "It's time to end for today, but I just want to say how glad I am you were with us, Bud." That was an understatement.

At Thanksgiving, I went to the day treatment center ready to carve the turkey, as I have done for years. When I arrived, Jennifer remarked, "Beware, here's Nancy with her electric knife. This is the one time she can let out her aggression!" I was glad for the humor because I was missing Bud. Knowing he loved the turkey skin, I had always put some aside some for him—but not this year.

A few weeks later, during one of our last visits, while he was still able to speak clearly and coherently, I asked him what he thought God cared about, what He wanted from His people, and what He wanted from Bud. "To follow up on what He plans for us," Bud replied; "He wants our behavior to be the message from Him."

By Christmas, Bud was not able to speak clearly. Nonetheless, staff members and clients visited him daily.

After his death, in addition to the church service, we had a service for him at the program. Here was a man who had, by the world's standards, been given a raw deal in life. But in the end he triumphed.

Following the service, the director told us that Bud had given him one last message for the community there: "Go and tell those people they are the best sons of bitches I have ever hung out with in my life."

Ditto, Bud.

The meaning of this incredible life continues to reverberate in mine. In "Dry Salvages," T. S. Eliot writes:

We had the experience but missed the meaning.
And approach to the meaning restores the experience
In a different form.[1]

On the contrary, I had the experience of Bud in my group and then the benefit of talking with him for hours. In thinking and writing about him, I continue to probe what he meant to me and to the other members of the day treatment community.

In his book *The Prophets*, Abraham Heschel says that what characterized the prophets of Israel was their authentic utterance, their intent on intensifying individual responsibility, their impatience with pretense or self-pity, their awareness that religion could distort what the Lord was demanding from human beings, and the fact that although they often seemed to have a message of doom, they always ended with a message of hope.[2] For me and for the other members of the group that captures Bud.

Before I met him, I had been in religious life for forty years. I was part of the system; I talked the talk and walked the walk. But when I met Bud, he challenged me consistently. What did I think was God's will? How could a loving God mete out so much suffering? What did Jesus do for the hidden years of life?

Before Bud died, he said, "I am not trying to alter myself. I can't find myself being any different from the way I have always been. I have to concentrate on living, not with anger or bitterness, because that will drive people away."

It is such a demanding task not to alter yourself in relation to others or when illness is consuming you. In his darkest days as well as his brighter ones, Bud was always gracious, attentive to the needs of others, and grateful. From my early years in religious life, I felt I had altered myself to some extent in relation to others: Bud called on me to be more authentic in both word and deed.

When he asked, "What kind of a God would give someone a life like this?" I couldn't answer and thought of a quotation I once heard: "The question is not whether there is a God but whether God is compassionate."

Following Bud's death, I asked myself frequently where God's compassion was in Bud's life. In the past I might have rattled off some theological explanation, but for Bud's sake, whatever explanation I found had to come from my heart.

I think I would now answer that God's compassion was in Bud's compassion. Bud found God in the little children clutching their rope, in caring for his niece, in the stamps on a letter, in a shelter on a rainy day. What Bud taught me is that God, a Spirit, a Source of energy, is in the midst of the pain, in the ability of someone like him to persevere over a lifetime of illness with integrity and generosity of spirit. In that way he was like Beverly, although their journeys were so different.

Unlike Beverly, Bud didn't need the mental health professionals to integrate his spiritual quest with his illness. In being entrusted with his religious questions, his doubts, and his wisdom, I was privileged to know all of who he was and participate in his journey to wholeness.

5

The Role of Ritual

ne April day while standing in line waiting to buy coffee and a croissant at Au Bon Pain in Harvard Square, I heard, "Sister Nancy!" I turned around to see Bill, a client whom I had known at the state hospital eight years earlier. In addition to the Spiritual Beliefs and Values groups I initiated at the day treatment programs, I also led groups at one of the state hospitals from 1983 until it closed in 1989. With the exception of some individuals like Bill, most of the men and women were lifers, doomed to spend the rest of their days in a psychiatric institution.

As I greeted him, he said, "Do you still do that thing with the matzo crackers and bitter herbs?" He proceeded to tell me that he remembered the Seder service I had conducted for these very ill clients; it had meant a lot to him. Sadly, I told him that we had to give it up because of a mandate from the Department of Public Health that barred overt religious symbols and ceremonies. With a look of regret on his face, he said, "Too bad, Sister Nancy. That was a great service you did for us."

For me, the Jewish Seder had a long history. In 1968, while teaching at the Academy of the Sacred Heart in Cincinnati, Ohio, I tried to broaden the outlook of the girls in my high school religion class by giving them a taste of different religious traditions. At a time when our country was torn apart by dissension and turmoil, I wanted to help them become more tolerant and understanding of others. As part of this initiative, I invited a rabbi from the Hebrew Union College in Cincinnati to conduct a Passover Seder for my class.

The Seder meal commemorates Jewish liberation. The story in the book of Exodus recounts the journey beginning with the night on which the Angel of Death passed over the homes of the Israelites, whom God had warned to sprinkle the blood of the lamb on their doorposts. The Egyptians, who did not display the saving blood, lost their firstborn child. The following morning the Jews escaped from Egypt, commencing their long journey to the Promised Land.

But liberation was not achieved overnight. The forty-year passage was filled with challenges, resistance, community disputes, rebellion, hunger, thirst, and despair. The initial liberation and the arrival in the Promised Land were worthy of celebration, but as happens so often, the process tried the hardiest of souls.

In experiencing the Seder with the students, I realized that the Mass, as Catholics know it, is rooted in this ancient tradition. The relationship between the Seder meal and the story that was told on the night of Passover had new meaning for me as an adult. Growing up Catholic, during the Holy Week services we heard that Jesus was at a Seder meal when He offered Himself to His disciples, saying with the unleavened bread, "This is my Body," and with the final cup of wine, "This is my Blood, the Blood of the new covenant."

We listened to the story of the Exodus and how the Jews were liberated from the oppression of the Egyptians. The Jewish liberation from the slavery of the Egyptians was linked to Jesus freeing His people from the oppression of sin, both original and personal. But as a child, the story of Jewish freedom and any connection to sin meant nothing. In fact, I didn't really take in Jesus' Jewish identity.

At the Seder I shared with my students, I grasped the connection between the Jewish and the Catholic traditions; but I didn't see a more universal relationship for several years.

In 1976, when I was doing my postdoctoral internship in the psychiatry department of one of the Harvard teaching hospitals, the chair of the department invited me to a Seder at his home. Expecting a solemn, silent, reverent, and restrained ceremony, I was prepared to pray with my head bowed and my mouth shut, as I had learned to do in Catholic rituals.

Much to my surprise, I found myself at a real celebration, at a table beautifully set with flowers and the family's best china and silverware. The gathering was at first somewhat chaotic as guests arrived, bringing various dishes and finding a space for them on countertops already laden with the symbolic dishes of hard-boiled eggs, matzo ball soup, haroset (a mixture of apples and nuts), matzos, and parsley. Children argued over who would read the Four Questions and who would win a prize for finding the hidden matzo called the *afikomen*. Eventually, Rebecca, the mother of the family and the traditional leader of the Seder, announced that we would begin.

Solemnly, she lit the candles and said the first prayer, one that echoed back through centuries, a prayer said in times of persecution and in times of peace and abundance. "*Baruch ata Adonai*," it began, like so many Hebrew prayers: "Blessed are You, King of the Universe."

A guest named Sam interrupted the silence accompanying the prayer. He suggested that we skip the first few pages of the Haggadah (Passover prayer book) and get to the "good parts," like the plagues. One of the younger children wanted to get to the bitter herbs; another more observant adult wanted to do the whole service.

All the requests and preferences amazed me. Initially, I was very uncomfortable with this energy and outspokenness, having been taught that reverence and restraint dictated proper behavior at religious ceremonies. With effort I began to relax, after telling myself that this table fellowship was undoubtedly closer to the way Jesus celebrated the Seder. As the blessing was said over several cups of wine, it made sense that a little raucousness should be a natural accompaniment.

In addition to the humor, the bluntness, and the reverent irreverence, what affected me was that everyone present related the celebration to current events. We were not only remembering the Jewish deliverance from the slavery of the Egyptians but also present-day oppression and slavery all over the world, remembering it with anguish, longing, and prayers for the freedom of all people. There was a heartfelt connection between the suffering of Jews thousands of years ago and the suffering of people today. We were retelling the story but also adding a current one.

On my way home, I reflected on how much life was present in that celebration, how much history, how much community around the table, as well as a sense of community that extended beyond the confines of the home. The value of ritual and the importance of remembering took on new meaning.

I had been participating in this Seder for several years before I started my first Spiritual Beliefs and Values group in July 1981. The following spring I suggested to the director of the program that we have a Passover Seder. This was a truly preposterous idea—to offer a ritual with a specific religious connection in a psychiatric day treatment program, to be conducted by a Catholic nun, no less. To my knowledge, at that time nothing similar had ever been offered in a mental health setting.

In suggesting the Seder, I hoped to shed some light on the clients' suffering, to give some meaning to their pain, so they would learn that they were not alone on the journey to freedom. Even those clients who were involved in a religious community seldom saw a connection between their lives and the sermons preached from the pulpit or the altar. In fact, because of their illness, most of them had stopped participating in any organized religious observance.

Fortunately, both the director and the assistant director, who was Jewish and one of the vociferous staff skeptics, liked the notion of a Seder. They suggested inviting all the clients and staff, not just the members of the Spiritual Beliefs and Values group. We made it very clear that participation was voluntary so as not to violate any church-state boundary. Without reflecting on it, I was putting myself in the role of spiritual leader.

For two weeks prior to Passover, we discussed the Seder. At that time there were three Jewish clients in the group, including Betty, who had always been concerned that the Spiritual Beliefs and Values group was going to be too Christian. Betty had had a very solid Jewish education, spoke fluent Hebrew, and knew her Jewish history. She recounted to the other clients the history of Passover and explained the significance of the Seder.

Instantly, she was transformed from client to knowledgeable leader. No one had ever drawn on Betty's Jewish experience, nor had she attended a Seder for years because of her hospitalizations. To think that we were going to have a Seder was as astonishing to her as it was to me!

For the sake of the Christians present, I explained that it was at a Seder meal that Jesus had changed the bread into His Body, what we have come to know as the Eucharist. Historically, we were doing what Jesus, a Jew, had done.

On the appointed day, we gathered in the community dining room, where the table was neither set with fine china and silverware nor laden with rich food. With a white tablecloth, flowers, candles, and the "Seder plate," on which I had placed all the traditional foods—the lamb bone, the parsley, the roasted egg, the haroset, the matzos, and the horseradish—I tried to beautify an otherwise drab environment. Paper cups and paper plates were our tableware.

As the clients drifted in, there were exclamations: "This looks beautiful!" "What's that bone doing there?" "Are we going to eat all that stuff?" "Are we going to have matzo ball soup?"

I began with a brief explanation of what we were going to do and asked for volunteers to read. Since an authentic Seder is very long, I had shortened the ceremony and made some adaptations.

As I sat at the head of the table and looked around the room at the twenty-five clients and staff, I thought of our commonality. Clients and staff alike, we all wanted to move from whatever oppressed us to freedom. For most of those present, their personal journeys were truly like forty years in the desert, years of wandering in and out of mental hospitals, halfway houses, and day treatment programs. But no one had provided them with a context for the journey. In celebrating the Seder, these clients were no longer the marginalized "mentally ill." They shared a kinship with all the others trekking along the path to freedom.

To center ourselves and to calm the hubbub, I suggested that we spend a moment in silence before beginning. With great dignity and pride, Betty stood up to light the candles and said in a clear strong voice, "*Baruch ata Adonai . . . ,*" reciting a blessing she had not said in public for over twenty years. When she sat down, there was an unplanned moment of silence. Then Joshua and Andrea, the other Jewish clients, took turns saying the blessing in Hebrew over the matzo and the grape juice substituting for wine.

The Christians also took turns reading. We all dipped our parsley in the saltwater and ate the bitter horseradish with the haroset, remembering that life has bitterness and sweetness. One client passed on the horseradish, saying, "No, thanks. My life has enough bitterness in it already."

At one point I invited everyone to name other nations and peoples who also longed for freedom. The homeless, children with AIDS, South Africa, Northern Ireland, people with addictions, and Israel were some of the places and people cited. Betty ended the Seder with the final Hebrew blessing, no longer concerned that I was going to "make her Catholic."

Thus we established a new tradition. Yearly, we celebrated the Passover Seder, which became a salutary event eagerly anticipated by both clients and staff. Once a year, in this simple but meaningful ritual, the sufferings of the clients, their struggles and their perseverance, were seen in a universal perspective. In his classic book *Man's Search for Meaning*, Victor Frankl says:

> Whenever one is confronted with an inescapable, unavoidable situation, whenever one has to face a fate that cannot be changed, e.g., an incurable disease, such as inoperable cancer, just then is one given a last chance to actualize the highest value, to fulfill the deepest meaning, the meaning of suffering. Suffering ceases to be suffering in some way at the moment it finds a meaning, such as the meaning of a sacrifice.[1]

The week before celebrating our seventh Seder, I encountered an unexpected problem. As usual, I explained the significance of the Seder and discussed its relationship to the Christian tradition. When I had finished, Sarah, a new Jewish client, burst out, "That's the trouble with you Christians! You are always taking something that is ours and making it yours. Count me out."

Taken aback by her anger, I tried to give an explanation based on historical fact, but that didn't calm her. Though the group members spoke of the Seder's importance to them, she was not persuaded. Although we told her that participation was always voluntary, she took offense at the very idea of the ceremony. In her outburst, Sarah voiced one of the recurrent difficulties that shadow religious discussions. The overemphasis on what belongs "to us," rather than on what we have in common, can often lead to bitterness and resentment.

The following week, just before we settled around the table, Sarah approached me and asked if she could say one of the Hebrew blessings. Afterward, she said, "I really liked that. When we did the Seder at my house, I always thought it was too long and had no meaning. I got bored. But I really liked this one. It makes me get something about my life. Are we going to do it again next year?" I assured her that we would. With each celebration, the clients deepened their appreciation of the Seder's significance for their lives.

Then one year, much to my dismay, a representative from the Department of Public Health appeared. Responding to a client's complaint about the presence of a menorah (the eight-branched candlestick used at Hanukkah), the DPH representative came in to assess whether we honored religious freedom in both the day treatment program and in the Social Club program, an afternoon and evening program that shared the same space. The client was a member of the latter.

In less than two hours, after interviewing only the day treatment staff and the Social Club staff—not me—he said categorically that all traces of anything with religious significance had to be eliminated. He did not interview a single client to assess reactions to the presence of the menorah, of a Christmas tree, or of the Seder celebration. By totally disregarding the clients, he could not ascertain if they felt that their religious freedom was being compromised, nor did he gain any understanding of the Seder's importance to them. Since attendance at the service was voluntary, the clients were absolutely free to participate or not.

Supposedly his role was to act on behalf of the clients and carry out the mission statement of the Department of Public Health. Earlier in this book, I described why mental health providers omitted any discussion of religion in treatment. But the DPH representative showed up in early 1992, when a growing body of research indicated that religious beliefs and religious affiliation could be beneficial to those who suffered with mental illness. Though the DPH rep may have been unaware of the research, he should have known that the 1992 standards for the JCOHA (Joint Commission on Hospital Accreditation, today known simply as the Joint Commission) state that the spiritual needs of the clients must be respected. Although the day treatment program was not a hospital, the fact that the

JCOHA, a government agency, was addressing the spiritual needs of the clients should have made him pause before making his decision.

If the Seder service had been mandatory, if proselytizing were occurring in the community, if diversity were not respected, the DPH representative would have been acting on behalf of the clients. But in this case he made a decision that was in direct opposition to what was meaningful, life-affirming, and community-building. Lacking leverage, the clients were given no voice in the decision. The actions of this bureaucrat suggest that he saw the clients as unable to discern between religious freedom and coercion. Again, the clients were victims of the stigma of mental illness; their thoughts and feelings were suspect.

Since nothing like a Seder was being done elsewhere in a mental health setting, the staff representative could appeal to no precedents. In attempting to safeguard the rights of an individual, the DPH allowed one client to impose her nonbeliefs on an entire community.

When the clients heard that we were forced to cancel the Seder, they were more outraged than the staff. Bud was among the angriest. Deprived of one of the most meaningful events of the year, they wanted to protest, but the director of the center felt that doing so could jeopardize our funding. So we acquiesced, once again with a sense of powerlessness, an all too familiar feeling for those who suffer from mental illness.

I find it curious that when national tragedies occur, such as the Columbine shootings, the Oklahoma bombing, 9/11, Hurricane Katrina, or the shootings at Virginia Tech, rituals that offer meaning, connection, and solace are held for people of all religious persuasions. It is assumed and understood that rituals are appropriate; government officials do not object. But when a ritual that can offer meaning, connection, and solace is held for those who suffer from mental illness, a government agency objected. In this instance I wasn't able to influence the decision, nor was I given the opportunity to educate the representative. The education of mental health professionals has been an ongoing challenge for me.

The Seder was not the only service I have initiated. During the first year I worked at the state hospital on a locked ward, one of the patients committed suicide. Because these patients were restricted to the ward unless they had earned privileges, they could never attend a religious service in the chapel when a patient died. Having spent years together, the patients were like family to each other, yet at the time of a death, they had no ritual by which to focus their grief. Apparently no one, not even the hospital chaplains, ever thought of acknowledging a patient's death on the locked wards. I suggested having a memorial service on the ward for the person who had killed herself.

When I proposed the memorial service at a staff meeting, the faces of those present registered shock. This reaction was similar to the reaction when I proposed the Spiritual Beliefs and Values group at the day treatment program. Some staff members gulped audibly.

One person said, "Are you serious? With this population? They won't be appropriate" (a term the clients detest).

Another chimed in, "Too many are delusional."

Someone else contributed, "We have never done anything like this before."

"Many of the clients here are suicidal," voiced another, naming the real fear. "What if the service prompts someone to kill himself or herself in order to have a service and gain some recognition?"

Some of the staff had worked with these men and women for twenty years. What did I know about leading a service for people who were "crazy"? I was just a nun-psychologist, an outsider, who dropped in once a week. But for me, being "crazy" didn't exclude having normal feelings about death, about losing someone you had known for years, about the need to mourn.

Though a suicide was endlessly processed from a psychological point of view in therapy groups at the hospital, a service was unheard of. With many unknowns and more than a little trepidation, the staff agreed to the service. They planned for sufficient coverage to control any outrageous behavior.

A week later, a terribly hot day in August, staff and clients gathered in the community room, a large room with cream-colored walls that had not seen a paintbrush in years. We sat in ugly institutional chairs with torn vinyl seats that were scattered throughout the room. A blaring TV, barred windows, and a pervasive cigarette odor completed the décor of this less than sacred space.

Some patients talked to themselves or to their inner voices; some sat and stared; some thumbed through magazines, just as they always passed their endless minutes, hours, and days. No great cathedral, this—more like the trenches, an unseemly place in which to hold a service and remember a life.

As we arranged the chairs in a circle, we reminded people of the occasion and invited all who were interested to come and join us. Eventually, about thirty people assembled. Seated at a table with an attractive yellow cloth, a vase of flowers, a basket with a beautiful loaf of challah, a tape recorder, and a candle, I welcomed each one.

"Today we are going to have a memorial service for Libby," I said. "I know that many of you have known her for a long time, so we want to honor her today and grieve her death. We'll begin with some music."

A voice from the back row called out, "Are you going to play a John Denver song? She loved John Denver."

"No," I replied. "I didn't know she loved John Denver. I didn't know Libby very well. She only came to my group a few times."

Trying to remain steady and calm but feeling very anxious, I continued, "Thank you for sharing that about Libby. We'll have time later in the service to share more memories of Libby, but right now, I'd like to explain the rest of the service so that everyone knows what we are going to do.

"We'll begin with some music, followed by a reading from the New Testament, because Libby was a Christian. Then there will be a few moments of silence and time to share our feelings about Libby. After this, we will break bread as a sign that we all need to be nourished in the face of loss. We'll end with some music, and then we'll have juice and cookies."

Another voice yelled out, "Can we begin with the juice and cookies?"

One of the staff quietly explained that the food would come at the end.

As "Spring," from Vivaldi's *Four Seasons*, played, I sat there hoping that more voices, either internal or external ones, would not interfere with the music. With a sense of poignancy, I looked at the faces of the patients, faces that were empty, faces that were anguished, faces that seemed lost, faces suffused with a surreal serenity. I wondered about their lives and their histories, about what had brought these patients to this point and what had brought Libby to end her life. When the music stopped, two of the patients who had sat still for three minutes, exceeding their normal limit, got up quietly, walked to the back of the room, and began pacing.

One of the staff read the passage from the Gospel of John where Jesus comes to His disciples and says, "Peace be with you." I'd chosen that passage with the dual hope that Libby would now have peace and that this service would bring some peace to the clients and staff.

"Now we'll have a minute of silence, and then I'd like to invite you to share whatever you want to about Libby." Much to my surprise, we really did have a minute of silence. Upon this ordinarily agitated, noisy environment, a sense of quiet descended.

Not wanting to push my luck, after a minute or two—which seemed like ten—I said with my heart in my mouth, "Now anyone who wants to can speak about Libby."

"Libby liked John Denver. I gave her one of my John Denver tapes when we lived in the halfway house together. She was in love with him. I wish she hadn't killed herself."

From the corner of the room, another patient said, "She was a really kind person, but she was very sick. She'd share her cigarettes with me."

"But she shouldn't have killed herself. Didn't she know what that would do to the rest of us? Makes me f—— angry that she did that."

A staff person, trying to lower the bar, said, "She tried very hard all the years I have known her. She was in a lot of pain."

"We're all in pain," another said. "But we keep going. I did like Libby. She watched out for people."

"I think it's really sad that her life ended that way. I am going to miss her. She had a nice smile."

Sensing that no one else wanted to speak, I moved on: "In many religious traditions, people break bread as a sign of their togetherness, a sign of community. So now we will take this bread, and after I break it and give each person a piece, we will all eat it together."

This was like telling little children not to eat any candy from their Halloween bags until they got home. To my surprise, as I passed the bread, each person held it.

When I returned to my seat, we all ate. One or two people piped up: "Can we have another piece? That's good bread, better than the white cardboard we get here."

I assured them that after the service they could have more. Vivaldi's music filled the room.

What impressed me was that despite years of medications, of hospitalizations, of living in inner darkness, those who spoke did so with disarming honesty and clarity.

At the conclusion of the service, some of the staff that had been most anxious approached me.

The first person said, "That was amazing."

Another said, "I was really touched."

The staff psychiatrist said, "I have never seen the patients so attentive."

The last one chimed in: "Thank you. You took a big risk."

Since that first service more than twenty years ago, I have held numerous memorial services in various settings for men and women who have died due to natural causes, such as cancer or heart attacks, or to suicide. Memorializing a person who committed suicide has never led to another suicide.

All of us want our lives to be recognized by someone, to have a sense that we have made a difference, even to one person. One of Ralph Waldo Emerson's definitions of success is "to know that even one life has breathed easier because you have lived." Over the years I have learned how the Libbys of the world have brightened someone's day with just a cigarette, a kind word, or a smile and how crucial it is to acknowledge the ways in which a person has made a difference.

One year we had an unusually high number of deaths, most, but not all, due to cancer and heart attacks. To offset the services for mourning, I thought we needed to have a service that focused on life. Aware that the holidays are a painful time for many individuals in the day treatment programs, I designed a service that focused on light. We could thus honor the Jewish holiday of Hanukkah, which centers on lighting the menorah over an eight-day period of time; Christmas; the Solstice, with its rituals of light to drive out the darkness of the shortest day of the year; and Kwanza, the African American celebration of values. By focusing on the universal significance of light, I hoped to avoid another clash with the Department of Public Health.

For the light service, I invited each person to take a candle, place it in one of the wreaths, and name someone who had been a source of light for him or her in the past year. "My mother," "my boyfriend," "the staff," "John," "Janet," "my coordinator," "Beverly, who died," "Nancy," . . . The clients surprised me with their courage and kindness.

All the comments were from the heart. Quietly we sat together, observing the light and all it represents. We concluded with lines from Susan Cooper's poem *The Shortest Day*:

> *And everywhere down the centuries of the snow-white-world*
> *Came people, singing, dancing,*
> *To drive the dark away.*
> *They lighted candles in the winter trees;*
> *They hung their homes with evergreens;*
> *They burned beseeching fires all night long,*
> *To keep the year alive.*[2]

Eggnog and cookies concluded the service.

This service has become a focal point of the year for the clients, for it eases the pain of the holidays. To replace the Seder, I've also composed a "service of new life" for spring. Instead of the wreath and candles, we have flowers. As each person puts a flower in a vase, each one names some new life found in the past year or a person who has been a source of life.

"I have been sober for the year," said one client. Others added: "I have moved out of the shelter into an apartment of my own. My poems were published in *Spare Change*. My therapist; Bob; I started a volunteer job; Gail; AA."

Although the clients and staff enjoy the spring service, it has never replaced the Seder. It doesn't link them symbolically, as the

Seder did, to generations of men and women who have journeyed through life, moving from a place of bondage to a place of freedom. I have rethought the value of religious traditions. When they truly serve us, they take us out of ourselves and link us to something transcendent, fostering a sense that we are part of a larger whole.

For years as I conducted these services, I was extremely self-conscious. My voice was a little artificial. I prepared my script. I was in a role. I didn't feel totally comfortable in my own skin. Maybe this was due to my discomfort with my role as a nun in a setting where I wanted to be recognized primarily as a clinical psychologist. Maybe it was my uneasiness about the task at hand, as I never knew what would emerge from the gathered assembly. Maybe it was that I was still trying to find myself.

Who was I? A psychologist, a nun, a minister to the community—"Doctor Kehoe," "Sister Nancy," or just "Nancy"? However I might describe or define it, I was vaguely ill at ease as I led the services.

Curiously, it was only when I led the memorial service for Bud that I was aware of feeling completely relaxed and at one with myself. I sat in the middle of the sofa, in the same physical place where I had been sitting for years at all the other services; this time, however, I was in a completely new place inside my head. I recognized that I was the spiritual leader of this little community and had become comfortable with that role.

The image that comes to mind is that of a little girl who wears her mother's high heels and dress-up clothes. Then one day the shoes and the clothes are her own. They now fit. These men and women had become my little congregation, and I was their shepherd. I had become ordained, not in the sacramental sense but in the sense in which the early Christian community used the word—called forth by the community to serve the community.

In thinking about this, I looked up the meaning of ordination. The word *ordain* comes from a Latin verb meaning "to order or arrange." I had helped bring some order into the lives of these men and women, and they in turn helped me reorder my own inner life.

It hasn't just been the services that have helped individuals gain some order in their lives and enabled me to accept my role with them. Many who suffer from mental illness live with a personally defined dual diagnosis: "mentally ill" and "sinner"; they have two "disorders." Some, having had troublesome experiences with religious professionals, hesitate to seek out a priest or minister for forgiveness. Conversely, the mental health professionals deal with the illness of the clients but not with their sense of sin. Searching for peace, acceptance, and forgiveness, some have sought me out to make their "confession." The middle of a corridor in the day treatment program or outside in the designated smoking area is an unlikely place to hear someone's confession, but that is what has happened to me on repeated occasions.

One day after a group meeting, a client named Martha asked if she could speak with me. Martha is an attractive woman in her forties. Always impeccably, stylishly dressed, her hair pulled back in a French knot, her clear hazel eyes enhanced by just the right amount of makeup, Martha looks as if she works at the Gap or a trendy women's store. In the group, she brings up probing, philosophical questions that consume many of her waking hours when she is not overcome with feelings of self-hate, anger, guilt, and depression.

Just as her external appearance suggested a "tied-together" life, her family history also seemed solid, but there was an undercurrent, not visible to others, of emotional abuse, rivalries, and isolation. Scarred by this early history and searching for acceptance and love, Martha has led a tumultuous life. Numerous relationships, moves, and hospitalizations have taken their toll.

When she approached me, I didn't know much about her background other than what she had shared in the group.

But she wanted to speak with me, to tell me some of the awful things she had done. She wanted to know if she could be forgiven. Her striking eyes were filled with pleading. *Am I a real sinner? Will God forgive me for what I have done? How can I forgive myself?*

I had no magic words; I didn't even have sacramental words. But what I had was a heart that went out to this woman. For her I was a representative of God. I could hear what she was saying, and I could respond from the bottom of my heart: "Martha, I believe that God forgives you."

She was close to tears as she said, "Thank you. That brings me peace. You don't know how long I have felt like such a sinner, such a no-good person." Months have gone by since this encounter, yet she comes back to it, both in the group and when we meet.

On another day, Sam, who towers over me at six foot three, asked if he could speak with me. Sam has come to the group only sporadically but often talks to me as I come and go from the program. The first time I really connected with Sam was following a memorial service held for one of the clients at the Social Club. Sam had written a poem to express what Barry meant to him. The poem's simplicity, warmth, and humor captured Barry in a nutshell. Afterward I told Sam how impressed I was with his piece.

"Really, Nancy? Gosh, that's good of you to say that. I don't think what I do is worth much, so it means a lot to me that you say that."

Months after this service, Sam became a member of the day treatment program. One day after the group had concluded, he took me aside and said, "Could I talk to you sometime? I am really troubled."

"Sure, Sam," I replied. "I have some time right now."

We walked away from the smokers, and he leaned toward me with anguished eyes, and asked, "Do *you* think I am going to hell because I am a Jew? My brother has become a born-again Christian, and he says that anyone who doesn't believe that Jesus is his Lord and Savior is going to hell. I know I have done a lot of bad things in life, but do you really think I will go to hell if I don't believe in Jesus? Would God do that? My brother also doesn't get mental illness. He thinks if I believed in Jesus, I would be OK. This is so upsetting to me. I wonder if I am possessed by the devil."

With some anger in my heart at the way religious messages can cause such anguish, I said, "Sam, Jesus was Jewish. You won't go to hell for being faithful to your Jewish beliefs. Since your brother doesn't understand mental illness, maybe it's better not to get into these discussions with him."

"Thanks, Nancy; it's a relief to hear you say that. You know, one time I tried to be Christian, but it just didn't work. I am Jewish."

"You have to be what you are, Sam, and no one can tell us what we should be."

A smile came over his face as he said again, "Thanks. I may need to hear that again, but right now I am less afraid."

I walked to my car, feeling that I had heard yet another person's confession.

6

The Dilemma
of Voices

If you talk to God, you are praying. If God talks to you, you have schizophrenia" is a quote attributed to Thomas S. Szasz, a Hungarian psychiatrist. If we accept this as a truism, we can conclude that major religious figures such as Abraham, Moses, Samuel, Muhammad, Buddha, Mary, Jesus, and Mother Teresa were all "mad." All heard God's voice or experienced some kind of revelation that impelled them to dramatic action. I, too, heard a voice that impelled me to become a nun, a very dramatic action for me.

While a freshman in college, during a time of retreat—a spiritual exercise required in most Catholic colleges in the 1950s—I was kneeling alone in the chapel when I heard a Voice that told me to go to Kenwood, the house of formation for the Religious of the Sacred Heart. One might say it was the boot camp for nuns. I was aghast. Even as a little girl, I'd heard about Kenwood from an aunt who was a member of the Religious of the Sacred Heart. But I was an eighteen-year-old college freshman who wanted a life. I didn't want to believe what I'd just heard.

Appalled, with tears streaming down my face, I remember saying, "Not my will, but Thine be done." My whole young life, my parents had taught me that our purpose here on earth is to do God's will. But this was too much. I never wanted to be a nun. I wanted to be a nurse, to get married and raise a family.

I sat there sobbing, but felt I had no choice. Because the Voice was so clear and the message so specific, I never doubted that somehow it was the Voice of God. I hated the idea so intensely that I resolved to tell no one. I intended to keep dating and having a good time, determined to squeeze every precious and pleasurable moment out of what little life was left to me.

In March that year my grandfather died, and I returned home to Chicago for his funeral over the Easter break. One night as my family sat around the kitchen table, my older brother asked, "What are you going to do with your life? You're just playing around in college, not focused on anything." He was right: I was a party girl, not an academician, and had no intellectual ambitions.

To everyone's amazement, I said, "I am going to Kenwood."

My mother, who had just lost her father, was being told in a somewhat cavalier way that now she was going to lose her only daughter to a cloistered life. She was devastated. My father was more pragmatic and thought that if this was what I needed to do, I should do it. I didn't tell them about the Voice. I didn't tell anyone. When I think back on this, I find it amazing.

I wasn't questioned more about my decision.

Over and over in religious traditions, we encounter the phenomenon of a "voice," a "knowing," an "epiphany." Were all these men and women, myself included, crazy?

Twenty-five years after hearing this Voice, I met many women and men at the day treatment program who wrestled with the dilemma of voices. Given my religious background and my personal experience, I became intrigued with how the clients determined the difference between the voices that are a symptom of their illness and voices they claimed were something "other." Unlike many mental health professionals, I didn't assume that all voices are part and parcel of their disease.

I began to wonder how we discern which voices are constructive and which are destructive? Are some the Voice of God? Are they all symptoms of illness? What do the voices prompt us to do or to believe? What difference does it make for treatment to consider the possibility of different kinds of voices? The skeptic might ask whether a more positive voice is simply the individual's own healthy voice.

In wrestling with these perplexing questions and my persistent desire to understand my Voice better, I interviewed Beth and Taylor, two members of the day treatment program who have been besieged by auditory hallucinations and also claimed to have had a religious experience.

A short, heavy-set woman, Beth is always meticulously groomed and wears attractive, brightly colored clothes. Frequently she comments on what I wear, sometimes quizzically and with a twinkle in her eye: "I like your earrings—but I didn't think nuns wore earrings."

I assured her that though most didn't, this one does. The twinkle in her eye, her pleasant appearance, and the gentle tone of her voice are only one side of Beth; violent rage, anxiety, and voices comprise a darker side. Beth grew up in Brooklyn with two brothers, a sister, and two alcoholic parents, "the usual alcoholic family," an umbrella phrase she uses to signify the chaos, unpredictability, secrecy, isolation, and repression of feelings characteristic of alcoholic families. "Dad's getting tired" was her family's way of referring to the fact that he was drunk.

To escape, she spent a lot of time on her own and found some salvation in school, where she was very popular and athletic, excelling in tennis, bowling, softball, and archery. Fascinated by stories about Indians, as a young child she made herself a bow and arrow and practiced archery in the backyard until an arrow nearly grazed a neighbor. I smiled as I pictured a little girl shooting arrows across a fence and a surprised neighbor ducking, wondering if he was seeing things.

After graduating from college with a major in English and education, she joined the Peace Corps, not for totally altruistic reasons: it was a way out of her chaotic home. She was assigned to teach English in an elementary school in Turkey for two years.

At twenty-one she faced forty middle school children in a classroom. With no teaching experience, unable to speak Turkish, and feeling anxious and alone, Beth struggled to do her job, but the pressure became too great. During the day her anxiety manifested itself in bouts of anger with her students and in an inability to organize her work. At night she walked in her sleep. Within a year she broke down, admitted she could not continue, and was flown back to the States with a staff doctor from the Peace Corps.

Hospitalized in Washington, D.C., she was put in a quiet room:

> All I could do was cry. In an interview with the head doctor,
> I explained I had to go back to Turkey. I had always finished
> what I started. When his response was negative, I went berserk,
> got violent, and totally lost control. I was beating on people and
> beating my fists against the wall so hard they bled. So they gave
> me massive doses of thorazine, which put me in a constant daze.
> Because they were afraid of my violence, I spent a lot of time
> in the quiet room, where there was one window. I spent hours,
> days, watching the trees change. Finally I was discharged, but
> I never returned to Turkey.

For periods of time she would do well before extreme anxiety or violent outbursts overwhelmed her. In the 1960s and 1970s, the treatment in mental hospitals for anxiety and violent behavior was to wrap the patient in cold sheets or put the person in a warm bathtub with a vestlike garment up to the neck. On two occasions, Beth attempted suicide. The radio cord she had tied to a showerhead broke just as she was losing consciousness. On the verge of dying, she thought that God had saved her for a reason. When I asked her what she had been saved to do, she confided, "To help people in need. I want to make their lives easier, to let them know they are not alone."

Between hospitalizations, she was engaged to an army officer. Shortly after he was sent to Okinawa, she followed him with wedding dress and veil in tow. Once there, she realized she didn't love him enough to marry him. When familiar feelings of loneliness, anxiety, and fear overcame her, she was put in the psychiatric ward of a military hospital before being flown back to the United States on a medical plane with the wounded from Vietnam. Years later she vividly recalled the voice of a young wounded soldier strapped down next to her who kept reassuring her that she was going to be OK. Very lucidly and with an admirable objectivity, she described these painful years to me, proof that mental illness does not destroy a person's intellectual and emotional capacities.

Despite numerous hospitalizations, Beth leased a studio apartment and worked as a home health aide, a job she loved because she enjoyed helping older people. Recognizing this aptitude, she applied to graduate school in social work. With one look at her psychiatric history, the registrar recommended that Beth work in a floral shop, a low-stress job. Devastated, she went home and lay on the couch, where, desperate and sad, she prayed to God for help.

Feeling stronger, she returned the next day to talk to the registrar. With a fierce determination, Beth insisted that she be allowed to apply. Not only was she accepted, she earned her master's of social work degree and landed a position in a senior housing facility. Her determination reminded me of Beverly, who completed her college degree at the age of forty-one.

In addition to her other troublesome symptoms, Beth has struggled with auditory hallucinations. But she maintains that she has also heard a different voice, the "Voice of God":

> The voices of my illness are frightening. They say, "Kill yourself. Kill, kill—you are bad." Or they tell me to hurt myself or someone else. Present much of the time, they torment me and take over my head. They are like waves crashing against my brain, so violently and so relentlessly. It's like having a boom box in your head you can't turn off, one that is blaring all these negative messages.

But then there is a voice that says to hang on, that "I am here. I won't abandon you." I feel it in my heart. I have a human bond with Jesus that I don't broadcast. I keep these things to myself. If you're a psychiatric patient and you talk like this, people think you are crazy. So many times in the mental hospitals, I have felt so alone; I'd sit on the cold floor and talk to God. I talk to God all the time. When I was overseas, I talked to God as if He were right next to me. That was the only comfort I had.

Despite all my years in religious life, I haven't always had a sense of a bond with Jesus. But on a few occasions, often at times when I was feeling bereft, I've had a sense of Jesus saying, "Peace is my gift to you." I may have been feeling desperate, but I never had to deal with the damning voices that have plagued Beth and Taylor.

In appearance Beth and Taylor could not be more dissimilar. Taylor looks much younger than her sixty years. Her short, slightly purple-tinted hair, her slim figure, and her "flower child" outfits belie her age.

Like Beth, Taylor grew up in a dysfunctional family, but Taylor's family was more rigidly religious. Both parents were college graduates. Her father was a mechanical engineer, and her mother had a degree in child development. Her mother's fervent religiosity, which she forced on her four children, combined with physical and emotional abuse, left Taylor a confused, frightened, and isolated kid. She described feeling like a "throwaway kid" by the age of eight. Like Beth and Beverly, Taylor worked hard in school. Academic success gave her some sense of self-worth. But the social side of school was agony. She had no friends and felt like an oddball. For comfort, she read her Bible every night and underlined the parts that gave her solace.

Looking back, she believes she had undiagnosed psychiatric symptoms: paranoia and dissociative experiences. (These are periods of an altered mental state, not uncommon in cases of abuse. By disconnecting, the psyche attempts to separate from

the painful reality of what is happening in the moment.) In college, Taylor rebelled against any notion of religion. Though still
uncomfortable around people, she managed to graduate.

She then went to New York with a boyfriend. When that
relationship ended, she returned to her family in Iowa and taught
English in a local high school. Like Beth, she couldn't handle
the classroom. Feeling frightened, alone, and ill at ease with her
family, she returned to New York, where she worked as a medical secretary and then at a university library until her depression
overwhelmed her.

> The blackness and the hopelessness of the depression felt so
> awful; I was afraid; I wasn't sleeping; I felt so alone and desper-
> ate that I seriously injured myself and ended up on the psychi-
> atric unit of a local hospital. Later I was committed to the state
> hospital because I was acting out and needed more restraints.
> I figured I deserved to be there because I was harming myself,
> which was a sin.

This was the first of many hospitalizations for Taylor.
During one of them she had a spiritual experience, which she
believes can go hand and hand with psychosis.

> I was afraid that I was going to hurt myself—and then I had a
> sense that God was with me. For three weeks, I was in a place of
> peace. I understood that everything is part of God's plan for us.
> I got a lot of insight into my family life. Even though I had a
> sense of God, I was still very frightened. Maybe I thought I was
> going to die. It was like holding two different realities together at
> the same time.
>
> If they want to say that was psychosis, they can call it
> whatever they will, but that is just their vernacular. They should
> call us prophets. In some countries, they call mad people proph-
> ets. For me, it was like everything fell into place: everything was
> there for a reason and made sense.

I have heard voices—in fact, I was tortured by voices for two years. I know what that is like and I know the difference. Chronic hallucinations are terrible; they just take up your mind. With them, sometimes I became violent.

God doesn't explain everything to us. I know I have a rational mind and a spiritual mind. I know I can also get misguided. When I think God wants me to commit suicide, I know I am misguided. With meds, I can be more rational, less emotional. I am clear about not being guided in the wrong way. Yet even with meds, I haven't mistrusted my experience. In this country, they can call religious experience what they will. I know when I am being guided along the way.

What intrigues me is that Beth and Taylor distinguish between the symptoms of their illness and their spiritual experiences. Both of their lives are more stable now, with meds that control their moods, with support systems in the community and secure housing. But when life is too challenging, they can become overwhelmed and angrily wrestle with the burden of integrating their spirituality and their symptoms.

From a strictly psychological point of view, the spiritual experiences that Beth and Taylor described could be understood solely as part of their illness, distortions of their minds. After all, given that they have a serious psychiatric disorder with auditory hallucinations, some would say that their perceptions shouldn't be trusted.

In contrast, when a person with cancer describes a sense that everything is part of God's plan, that person is listened to empathically, often with love, admiration, and respect. In fact, current research shows that faith makes a positive difference for individuals who suffer physical ills. The expression of faith is not deemed a symptom and dismissed as part of the illness. In the popular book *Tuesdays with Morrie*, Morrie says, "I'm bargaining with Him up there now. I'm asking Him, 'Do I get to be one of the angels?'"[1] The author did not conclude that Morrie was crazy.

While writing this book, I had eye trouble and couldn't wear one contact lens for a week: one eye saw distance, the other proximity. Both saw, but differently. That experience gave me direct insight into one way I see and listen to the clients, with one eye and ear focused on the psychological and the other eye and ear on the spiritual or religious. My eyes and ears adjust so that they can attend to the immanent, which is up close, or the transcendent, the beyond. I see and listen with eyes that adjust for perspective and ears that are attuned to different sounds.

But what if I were a skeptic—an atheist or an agnostic? What if I denied the possibility of a God or a spiritual reality and could only consider Beth and Taylor's voices as benign, wish-fulfilling delusions? Since the stance of disbelief is the position most clients expect from their caregivers, the clients are unlikely to reveal the experience of another voice.

But if even a skeptical, unbelieving therapist could consider the possibility that an individual has a sense of an internal life-giving voice even in the midst of chaotic, hallucinatory experiences, the therapist could explore it with the client.

So Beth and Taylor might be asked if they ever have a sense of something hopeful when they are besieged by destructive voices, and if so, how would they describe it? What does this sense enable them to do? Even a nonreligious therapist can be prepared for the client's references to God. Then the question is whether or not the therapist can willingly suspend disbelief sufficiently to explore the client's experience.

Trying to make sense of voices or one's inner experience is not a new phenomenon. For centuries spiritual and religious traditions have offered guidelines for discerning good spirits from bad spirits. (In a religious context the word *spirit* is used, not *voice*. In the Gospels, the mad are brought to Jesus to be healed from their possession by bad spirits.) To understand whether the voices the clients claim to hear are destructive or constructive, and to understand my own Voice and other religious experiences, I use these guidelines: What was the experience? What name does the client give to the phenomenon? What name did I give it? Does the name we give it affect how we hear it? Does the person deny other parts of his or her life (for example, that he or she has an illness)? Where does the experience lead? Can the client entertain questions about the experience? I explored these questions in the context of my whole life when I was in therapy and later when I was in analysis.

In *The Varieties of Religious Experience*, William James wrote, "The roots of a man's virtue are inaccessible to us. No appearances whatever are infallible proofs of grace. Our practice is the only sure evidence, even to ourselves, that we are genuinely Christian."[2] In other words, "By their fruits shall you know them." The veracity of a person's experience can be seen in how the person lives. Beth and Taylor spoke of spiritual experiences; in Beth's case she heard the words "I am here; I will not abandon you." Taylor had a sense of God's plan, a sense that everything would be OK. Taylor's experience sounds similar to that of Julian of Norwich, a fifteenth-century mystic who quotes from one of her divine encounters: "All shall be well, and all shall be well, and all manner of things shall be well."[3]

For Beth, the voices of her illness urge her to destructive actions, to hurt herself or others. Though medication helps, when she is in the grip of the voices, she feels besieged. The voice that she identifies with God, on the other hand, gives hope and a semblance of peace. Are both voices hers? Is what she described as God's voice her own strength that she couldn't identify or claim then but that had been there during many painful years?

Beth's sense of God's being with her enabled her to keep going and to minister to the elderly, which is what she is doing now in an assisted living facility. Taylor's experience allowed her to gain a different perspective on her family and to forgive them.

My Voice has led to a rich, full life I never would have imagined possible.

Several years ago at a presentation at the American Psychological Association's annual convention, when I talked about the Voice I had heard, I expected skepticism and criticism. To my surprise, I encountered neither. After the presentation, many psychologists in the audience approached me and shared personal stories that involved a sense of something "other." It became evident that many other people have had spiritual experiences they couldn't explain—some verbal, others nonverbal.

For fear of judgment within their professional communities, they remain silent. If fear silenced the professionals, how much more frightening is it for those who carry a diagnosis of mental illness to speak out?

In discerning voices, we are too easily limited by a single perspective. Considered alone, either the psychological or the spiritual may be limiting at best and injurious at worst. We know of tragic cases where a parent killed a child or a minister abused children "because God told them to do it"—in some cases with the support of the community.

In trying to make sense of a voice, such things as understanding the cultural context and the person's history, experience, and sense of community are all critical factors. Taylor addressed the need for more than one perspective when she said: "I, no, *we* have a spiritual mind and a rational mind."

Earlier I made reference to one of Bud's comments: "In people's backyard, around this corner, there are people with mental illness, people who are suffering, trying to find God in this. The world is finally paying attention—the medical people do not have all the answers."

Neither Beth nor Taylor claimed that the experience, the knowing, or the voice had taken away the pain of their illness, but it grounded them. It didn't lead to self-aggrandizement or displays of entitlement. Each woman allowed me to question her experience but also made it clear that she didn't share it with her mental health caregivers because she feared that it would be branded a "delusion." Both women believed that their therapists would only see them as sicker and that their honesty would work against them. For years I, too, never shared the story of my Voice. Given a therapeutic community that pathologizes or ignores the spiritual and the religious, with whom can people like Beth and Taylor confide about their spiritual encounters?

More often than not, they speak to no one. Some clergy still believe that if people had enough faith, they wouldn't be sick, and communicate this belief to their congregations. Unable to share their religious experiences with religious professionals, the clients have only themselves to trust. One said, "I know the difference between my voices and God. With my voices, I feel a sense of 'dis-ease'; I don't want to take my meds; I want to leave treatment, feeling I can go off on my own. With God, I feel a sense of peace; I can reach out for help."

Beth and Taylor held on to a core sense of who they were, a personal truth they would not relinquish. From my perspective, it strengthened them. Although I am a person with faith, I am not concerned with defending whether the voice was God's or their own. What is important to me is how they interpreted and used their experience.

External voices, not just internal ones, can foster strength and hope or hopelessness and a sense of limitation. The soldier on the plane kept reassuring Beth that she was going to be OK, that she would make it. Was that like the Voice of God? The registrar told Beth that she should work in a florist shop and forget about pursuing a social work degree.

A colleague of mine diagnosed with schizophrenia was hospitalized and suicidal at the time of his first breakdown. As he approached the room where he had planned to take his life, he cried out desperately, "Help." For a minute he stopped, then turned around and went back. He felt that something or someone had heard him.

When he woke up the next morning, he knew he wanted to live and to help others as desperate as he had been. Shortly after this, in his weekly meeting with his therapist, he was asked to name his goals. He said he wanted to use his Ph.D. to become a writer and help others. The therapist's response was that he was deluded and that he needed to focus on daily goals, like taking a shower. He was ill-advised to think of anything so grandiose.

A year later the voice of a second therapist told him to go for it. Today he is the vice president of a company, has written numerous articles on mental illness, and has started over five hundred self-help groups for men and women who suffer with a psychiatric disability.

When the voices of parents, ministers, teachers, and caregivers fall on the ears of people in a vulnerable position because of their illness, they have the potential to be as harmful as internal voices. The voices of others can limit us, define us, and instill guilt and fear. In the day treatment program, it is often the voices of the clients as well as the staff that offset the negative voices heard for years from parents, family members, teachers, and ministers or the internal voices of one's illness.

A vignette from one of our group sessions illustrates this.

Phil: I don't want to be here today. You guys are all calling me nigger. You don't like me. You want me outta here.

Rob: Phil, that's not true. I don't want you out of here. I gave you a cigarette this morning.

Chris: I called you over the weekend. You didn't think I hated you then, did you?

Phil: But you call me nigger behind my back. You talk about me.

Judy: Phil, we don't talk about you behind your back. Those are your voices that are telling you that. You're upset. Remember that last week we watched TV together in the Social Club?

Me: Phil, I wonder if you can hear what the others are saying to you. They are asking you to remember when they helped you out, or spent time with you.

(Short period of silence)

Phil: So you don't hate me.

Chris: We don't hate you. We want you here.

Phil: *(quietly)* I was feeling really scared this morning. When that happens, my paranoia takes over. I hear all these damning voices telling me, "All these people hate you; they hate you." Thanks, you guys. I hear that you don't hate me.

The voices of others can inspire us, encourage us, and give us hope.

7

Wrestling with God

For years I struggled to find balance between the part of me that is grounded in prayer and the longings of a woman who desires a spouse and family. More than once I considered leaving religious life with a view to getting married. Often I asked myself what my life might have been like if I hadn't listened to the Voice that called me to Kenwood. In analysis I'd examined the Voice that instructed me to go to the convent from every possible psychological angle and still believed that it had something to do with God. But in many ways I was like the elder son of the parable, the one who stayed at home doing what he thought his father wanted, but not whole-heartedly, probably envious of the younger brother, the prodigal son, who'd left home with his inheritance.

Overall my self-image was that of a person who loved life in its various manifestations. In times of retreat and in solitude, I experienced peace, contentment, and satisfaction. I held posi-tions of authority within my religious order and was an accom-plished professional woman. Yet all the while I knew I didn't fully possess the peace that defines wholeness.

When I made a thirty-day retreat after my mother's death, I became aware of latent anger I had harbored toward God all these years for calling me to religious life. With her death I had to face the concrete reality that there was no place I could call home: I had no spouse, no children or grandchildren who would be there for me. For a religious, the death of the last parent sharpens the reality of one's choice in a dramatic way.

In the summer of 2006, I took a month off to work in solitary splendor. I am blessed with a lot of energy; I am also cursed with the all-too-human gift of guilt. To make up to my community for my absence, I took on several house projects and also offered to help some of my religious sisters move. I said yes to everyone who needed my assistance, setting no limits. The self-imposed, limitless giving went on for two and a half months.

As I continued this frenzy of activity and tried to write this chapter, I became aware, not for the first time, of a sense of deprivation. I was angry and resentful at God for calling me to religious life, which required me to lose myself for the sake of others. I envied my brothers and some of my friends for their trips with families, their vacation houses, and their opportunities. In the world around me I saw violence, natural disasters, war, and church and corporate scandals.

Closer to home, there were the realities of religious life: an aging group of women, fewer women entering, increasing health care costs for the older religious, and financial stress. The expectations I had of life, of religious life, and of myself were once again being called into question. Like the psalmist, I cried out, but there was no response. After giving my life to God, now I felt abandoned and lost. All I could experience was a sea of painful emotions. Immersed in emptiness, I was minimally aware that these all-too-familiar emotions often overtake me when I have neglected my spirit, as I'd done that summer. A break I'd counted on to get back a sense of myself didn't materialize after a friend took a bad fall and needed my nursing care for a week.

When my brothers and I were growing up in Chicago and complained about the lack of something, my mother would always say, "The sun is shining and you're not in County Hospital." Chicago's County Hospital was as low as you could go. But as I tried to repeat my mother's mantra, it didn't alleviate what I was feeling. It also didn't alleviate the pain to remind myself that I had chosen to say yes to God. God had not forced me into religious life, and God was not forcing me to say yes to everyone and everything. Yet I chose to be angry with God rather than looking at the ways I needed to take better care of myself. As Bud said, "God wants us to be more responsible." But I wasn't there yet.

Instead, I spiritualized it all. I kept telling myself that this process was about purification, a stage all spiritual writers speak about; but it is one thing to read about it and another to experience it. I hated where I was. I couldn't connect with God, and I denigrated myself for lacking a sense of faith and trust.

Looking for opportunities that would relieve what I was feeling, I spent time with friends and family, but that only made me feel worse, because it highlighted what I didn't have. My analyst once said, "For you, to live is to compare." He was right: I am forever comparing myself to others, never to my advantage.

All summer I conducted my groups. Each Monday morning I parked my car in the school lot. As I approached the scarred and battered exterior of the building, I was greeted by the usual group of smokers, glad to see me again. My emptiness didn't seem apparent. In fact, the warmth of their greetings brought a smile to my lips. Here were people to whom I meant a lot. These people were not in County Hospital, but they weren't too far removed, and I was grateful to be with them—not exactly what my mother had in mind. I wasn't grateful because I didn't have a mental illness; I wasn't comparing myself to the clients and feeling better because I was healthy. I was simply grateful for them.

Entering the community area, a client who often repeats himself announced in a loud voice, "Nancy Kehoe is here. Nancy Kehoe is here. If it's Nancy, it must be Monday." The predictable greeting warmed my heart.

One week during this bleak summer, in a discussion on suffering, one of the members of the group said to me, "You don't have any suffering in your life. You don't have mental illness."

Another said, "Nancy must have some suffering in her life. She couldn't do this work if she didn't know some suffering. Mental illness isn't the only kind. We don't know what pains her, and we shouldn't. But she knows how to use her suffering. She is incredibly disciplined, and that is why she can do this."

Later this woman came over to me and said, "You are looking very tired. I worry about you. You have to take care of yourself. You mean a great deal to us, and I don't want to see something happen to you." I went to my car and wept.

Somehow, with these men and women, week after week, I found the soft spot in my heart, as the Buddhists say, the place where we can let our hearts be open and be touched by the suffering of others, where we can know compassion and a sense of connectedness. It was as though a little window opened in my heart for a brief time on Monday, but for the rest of the week, I closed it. I didn't want to be open to the suffering of others, nor did I want to be open to their joys. I wanted to be miserable. As I battled my own demons (envy, regret, guilt), the clients had a different perspective.

Toward the end of a discussion one day, one of the members of the group said, "It's not just the terrible things that happen in the world that make you doubt God, but also the terrible things that happen in your own life. But the fact that I'm alive today almost proves to me that there is a God. Sometimes it seems like in the worst times, God is closest."

I was even more in tune with her words than usual.

Later that afternoon I decided to go out to Walden Pond for a swim. I love the beauty of the small lake, the sense of being held by the tall pines that surround it. Crossing from side to side, I was deeply troubled by the fact that I'd spent so much of the summer in turmoil.

Once when I asked my father what he thought life was about, he said, "It's a learning process." At the time I thought he was referring to learning from experience: about people, situations, and events that will make you wiser, more compassionate, more accepting, and less idealistic but still hopeful. But now

I would add that a major part of the learning process is accepting who you are in order to be of service to others.

As I swam from one side of the pond to the other, I asked myself why going to the day treatment program made such a difference to me: Why was I at peace for two hours there on Monday? It was becoming clear to me that my exhaustion was due to the fact that I was trying to be Superwoman, all things to all people, and in the process had disused myself. I neglected the "love your neighbor *as* yourself" guide. Yet I sensed that there was more to my unease than just fatigue. My lack of peace was pointing to some warring factions within me, not just my management of some external realities. Even in national and international situations, real peace never happens until the core of the struggle is fully apprehended and addressed. A cessation of armed conflict does not result in peace. Real peace can be made only when the warring factions are fully and knowingly confronted.

During the ensuing weeks, my inner conflict raged on: What did I really want? Over time I began to see that making peace with my life meant dealing with my sense of loss on different levels. Ordinarily when we think of loss, we think of something or someone we've had, then lost: a person we loved, a dwelling place, an object, a sense of safety and security, something we knew and experienced. But I think we can also speak of loss as it relates to the choices we make, to our hopes, our fantasies, and our sense of self-worth.

In therapy I saw patients who grieved deeply after a parent's death not just for the loss caused by death but also for the loss of the parent they wished they had had. The death now put an end to that hope. I see my married friends dealing with a sense of loss in relation to their marriage—coming to grips with what won't be as they try to be present to what is.

Some of the pain I was feeling was related to what I felt I had lost by the choice I made. The loss was also connected to an unarticulated fantasy of what I thought a relationship with

God would be like—that I would have a sense of God's presence that would bring me peace, joy, contentment. Instead, for a long time I had felt none of that. Intellectually, I told myself that spiritual life is a process, that just as in marriages, relationships go through changes—and so must a relationship with God. But somehow my fantasy is that at least in a committed relationship, you have someone with whom to do battle. God is an elusive partner who doesn't speak up or talk back.

I didn't have what I seemed to want, and what I had wasn't what I thought I desired. Not being at home with myself, I also felt marginalized by others. The sense of loss, of not fitting in and being "other," was highlighted when I had lunch with colleagues. As we ate, each of them talked about their children. Feeling like I had become invisible, I interjected something about my love for children. Totally ignored, I was angry: I was a nun, not some disembodied spirit from outer space.

That night I had a dream in which I was figure-skating and singing a song from *A Chorus Line*, "What I Did for Love." I knew it was my way of sorting out the sense of loss I felt in relation to their conversation. I wanted to be seen as a normal person with human longings who was making a choice to live a celibate life not because I lacked other options but "for love."

If I were mourning what I thought would fulfill me as a person, what about the men and women I was working with? Mental illness robbed them of so much of what provides a sense of self-worth. Society's perception is that the "mentally ill" can't work, don't have healthy relationships, are to be feared, are not worthy of respect, and are relegated to the margins of society because they are "different." They are "worthless." Yet the men and women I know work tirelessly and valiantly to regain a sense of self that is lost with such a damning illness.

During one session a group member said, "I have thought of my sadness in having twenty-odd years of being mentally ill. That is a part of me. It's like taking a sad child in my arms and saying, 'It's OK to be sad. You have lost something.' I have to accept it and allow myself to feel the sadness, instead of fighting it."

Her comment reminded me of something Bud had said to me as he was coming to grips with all his losses:

> I want to die now; most of my life has been about survival. I've had no education, no girlfriend—no future. I look at my friends with their families and I think I should have gone along with them, but I was never able to catch up. I went from poverty into mental illness. I wanted to be a cop and work with juveniles or be a teacher. I have thought about taking my life. Losing my physical powers adds to the mental anguish. I've gotten over that because a lot of good people have come into my life since I have had a mental illness.

Don't fight, accept—this was the message. The whole summer seemed to be about understanding why I experienced a deep sense of self-acceptance when I was with the clients and felt unacceptable when I was "out in the world."

Finally I achieved a profound moment of enlightenment in a conversation with my client Russell after I'd confided in him about the Voice that told me, "I want you to go to Kenwood."

Russell fixed his kind eyes on me and said with Buddhist clarity, "Nancy, maybe that was deepest part of *you*."

Startled, I said nothing at the time. But his words kept echoing in me. At first I told myself, *No way—that was God, not me.* I continued to reflect on what he said and knew, deep down, that it was time to rethink my Voice. In some ways I've spent most of my religious life fleeing the Hound of Heaven—and myself.

My entrance to religious life more than hinted at a profound ambivalence about my choice. I had been seriously dating someone for three years at the time I made my decision. He was almost as surprised as I was when I told him, just weeks prior to my departure, that I was going to become a nun. Even on my way to the convent in Albany, New York, I veered off to party with friends who were spending time in New York City. My last five days before entering convent life were filled with what I must have imagined to be my final fling, nights at the Stork Club and Greenwich Village bars and even a horse-drawn carriage ride in Central Park.

Before taking the two o'clock train to Albany that last afternoon, I mailed my party clothes back to my mother. Traveling with a friend who was also going to Kenwood, we fortified ourselves with a few scotches.

At six that evening, dressed in a brown knit dress, a black pillbox hat, gold earrings, and several gold bracelets, detesting every minute of what I was about to do, I walked defiantly through the doors and into the great unknown of Kenwood, the Convent of the Sacred Heart, all because a Voice I'd heard instructed me to do this.

When the head of the formation program took one whiff of us, she told us we would spend the night in the guest rooms, "to sleep it off." The next day, with blazing dark eyes and a very stern countenance, she asked me why I had entered.

Through tears, I told her I thought this was the Will of God.

Coldly, she replied, "I don't think you even know who God is."

I know now that she could have sent me back to Chicago, as she had done with others. I've always wondered why she didn't.

The first months I spent in the convent were hell. My room was called a cell, fitting for someone who felt like she had landed in prison. I found out later that I had been given my own room instead of being in the dormitory because the nuns in charge were convinced I would be leaving in a few weeks.

Unlike other religious orders, until we received the religious habit, we wore our own clothes, not black skirts and white blouses. During my first weeks, every day after breakfast I was called aside: my skirt was too short, my sweater was too tight, my blouse was too sheer. This elimination of my wardrobe went on until I was left with few of my own clothes. The final straw came one Sunday when the assistant director told me I could not wear high heels. I was so angry I went back to my cell and kicked both heels into the ceiling. A substantial hole, unexplained for years, was my secret mark of defiance. Looking back, I don't know how I survived; it felt like I was being stripped of the things I valued and had so little to sustain me.

Nothing distinguished one day from the next. We had classes on religious life and the vows we would make at the end of the formation period. There was silence and more hours a day for prayer than I knew what to do with. Except for an occasional letter and phone calls on holidays, we had no contact with family. Talking in a casual way with other novices was strictly controlled. After hours of prayer and physical labor, "recreation" consisted of sitting in a circle and listening to the superior tell us what was going on in the world. We had no access to TV, radio, newspapers, or books.

Despite my acting out, I knew I was going to stay, not because I thought God would punish me if I left but because somehow this was what God wanted of me, even if I didn't want it for myself. I was convinced that this was God's will and that I was choosing, albeit reluctantly, to say yes.

In November we had a focused day of prayer, different from the other tedious days because there was more time for prayer and less for manual labor. To my surprise, I experienced a sense of peace in the presence of silence. Rather than attending to the significance of the peacefulness that came in the context of prayer, I shifted my focus outward. I stopped rebelling and began to accept and conform to all the rules, an act of obedience with serious detrimental effects.

Because I was so young, uncritical, and authority-conscious, I accepted what I was told and turned myself inside out to conform to it, totally repressing my former self. I didn't understand the relationship between the way we were told to live and how it fostered an inner life. Years later I gave a presentation at the American Psychological Association on the benefit of an ascetic life espoused from within as opposed to one imposed from without. I had learned the difference painfully.

After a probationary period of six months, those aspiring to religious life received the religious habit in an elaborate ceremony in which they entered the chapel in a wedding dress, a symbol of becoming a bride of Christ. Following the Mass, they left the chapel and donned the religious garb. What the nuns didn't know was that weeks before I left home, in anticipation of this event, I had already had my picture taken in my mother's wedding dress; my mother didn't think the convent photographer would take a good picture. In the portrait I look more like an aspiring movie star than an aspiring nun. By the time of the clothing ceremony, I knew I wouldn't be allowed to wear my mother's dress, which would clearly be considered too sexy. For years the portrait sat on my mother's marble table, along with the wedding pictures of my two sisters-in-law. Now it sits on my bookcase, a daily reminder of how naively I began this journey.

Once I donned the religious garb, I took on the persona of a nun and in the process became anxious, rigid, insecure, and scrupulous. After three and a half years of formation, I was sent out to teach. Clothed in the habit, I looked and acted like a good nun, but in truth I was a lost soul.

I was assigned to my first teaching job in Lake Forest, Illinois. Teaching little children was a nightmare; they can be like horses that recognize the rider's fear. An inability to articulate my inner confusion led to isolation and a sense of desperation. My hours of prayer were spent in tears, wondering how I could live the rest of my life in such misery.

Though I was depressed, no one, including me, recognized this fact. In weekly meetings with the superior and the principal, I was told that I had to grow up and to learn to control the children, but I had no idea how to do this. Even though I was miserable, I never thought of leaving religious life; in my mind, I was obeying the Will of God—at that point, an excruciating task.

After two and a half years in this failed assignment, I was sent to another school in Cincinnati, Ohio. I saw this move as a rejection. I felt like I had hit rock bottom. At twenty-five, my life was in shambles. I had entered a teaching order and couldn't teach. I had no friends, and my family had no idea what I was experiencing.

I arrived in Cincinnati afraid that my reputation had preceded me. A few days before school began, while preparing my second-grade classroom, a little girl came into the room, inquiring if I was to be the second-grade teacher. She was charming, and we hit it off immediately. Because she had a delightful laugh, I gave her the nickname "Giggles." Much to my surprise, the second graders in the class responded to me, and I to them: They were obedient, polite, and fun.

Weeks later I learned that "Giggles" had been suspended from kindergarten and first grade for various misdemeanors, including kicking one of the nuns in the shin. Thanks to Giggles's leadership of the class, we had a delightfully successful year. We have remained friends for over thirty years, which has given me the opportunity to share with her that I, too, had been a designated problem. Unencumbered by history, our first meeting transformed us both. I think this experience unconsciously influenced my decision never to ask about a client's diagnosis as a condition for becoming a member of the Spiritual Beliefs and Values group.

With this more positive experience of teaching, I began the very slow process of rediscovering the person I had been before

I heard the Voice. Help from some nuns and priests, along with modest success in teaching and working with students, as well as a period of renewal and a significant retreat experience, enabled me to gather some of the broken fragments of myself back into an integrated whole, or at least what I thought was whole at that point.

In my religious congregation, seven years after the period of initial formation, each nun went to Rome for six months of further formation before making a definitive commitment to God. Although Cincinnati had been a better teaching experience than Lake Forest, I still didn't know how to pray or what to do with periods of prayer that were not structured in a communal way. With five other nuns, I sailed from New York for Rome on the *Christopher Columbus* in September 1964. I remember only this: I was angry that we had to eat at the first seating, since the second seating was more glamorous. As the only one who didn't get seasick, I recall standing on the ship's deck, looking out at the expanse of the ocean, and feeling nothing. Unlike Jennifer, I did not see the hand of God in the glory of creation. I just felt empty.

The same woman who'd met me at Kenwood years before greeted us as director of the Roman program. This time there was no scotch on my breath. Vatican Council II, convened by Pope John XXIII to open up the Catholic church to the modern world, was in session. A revolution was in process.

During this second period of formation, a significant change occurred when I read Thomas Merton's *Seeds of Contemplation.* This was the first time I'd found an articulation of what I had been experiencing. Someone else had also known the sense of being lost, of emptiness. Again a voice, only this time it was Merton's voice, influenced me. His words opened a door and invited me into the world of prayer and contemplation. After seven years of wandering in my own internal desert, I finally discovered an inner world and knew a sense of peace and of wholeness. Apart from that November day of prayer in the novitiate, I had had no sense of an inner life. For the first time, I could honestly say that I was willing to embrace religious life.

Though her insights regarding prayer and contemplation were astute, the formation director in Rome still didn't read me correctly. One day I asked her, "Which is the real me, the me that loves Merton or the me that loves parties?" Her reply, "The you that loves Merton," was only partly true. The real me is both, but it took me many more years to discover this. In formation, I had lost myself in submitting to the dictates of religious life; now I was subscribing to her limited understanding of me, discrediting a truth I knew about myself.

In February 1965, I made my final profession in the Society of the Sacred Heart. But soon the religious life to which I was saying yes would change dramatically.

Since I still had not completed my baccalaureate, I returned to Duchesne College, the scene of the Voice, and graduated in 1965. With a college degree I could now teach high school and was sent back to Cincinnati. For the next four years, I taught French, history, religion, and English. I was dean of discipline and director of the drama department. With the rigid structures of religious life opening up because of the Vatican Council, our daily lives were more determined by our own choices than by external rules. I became more and more involved in my work with the students. Despite my "conversion" to the contemplative life that opened up in Rome, I gradually stopped praying. I didn't have time. The seeds of contemplation were being taken over by the weeds of activity.

In 1969 the formation director, who kept turning up in my life, arrived in Cincinnati and within a few days had sized me up. On a trip to the Abbey of Gethsemani in Kentucky, where Merton was buried, she told me that she thought I was lost again and that I needed to make a directed retreat. (A directed retreat is an extended period of silence and prayer and a daily meeting with the retreat guide.) She feared I would leave religious life: With the freedoms unleashed after the Council, many religious were doing just that. Her analysis startled me.

My interest in contemplation, my ability to be still for any length of time, my desire to have a relationship with God, all had dried up in the frenzy of activity. Knowing this, the retreat director, a priest, set out a very structured regime, not one that would be at the whim of my desires. For ten days I prayed six hours a day and met with him for an hour daily to talk about my prayer experiences. It was during those days that I had another experience of God, not a voice, but a "knowing."

One night I woke up and turned over on my back. Lying there, I had a sense that God's love would fulfill me as a person. Though it wasn't as though words were spoken, as in "I want you to go to Kenwood," for me the sense was clear. I felt a profound sense of *shalom*, the Hebrew word for peace that means more than peace—a sense of wholeness, of rightness. I remember thinking, *This must be what it is like to be loved by someone.*

After the retreat ended, I returned to Cincinnati to resume teaching. On the first day back, one of the students asked me what had happened: She said, "Your face has a glow, like you have fallen in love with someone."

The glow faded, and the sense that God's love would fulfill me as a person was challenged when a decision was made in February 1970 to close the school. I was devastated and angry, and I felt betrayed by the nuns in my religious order. Where was God in this for me? In a matter of months I had moved from a heartfelt sense of God's presence in my life to grave doubts, not an uncommon experience in a spiritual journey. It was a long time before I could answer my own question.

In the late 1960s one of the religious in my community who had received her doctorate in psychology from Boston College began doing psychological tests for the younger members of the order to determine what each one was qualified to do. Prior to this, religious did what was needed, which in some cases meant doing work for which they had little aptitude. I scored high on social sciences. Based on my scores in this category and the fact that this religious was a friend and role model, I chose to pursue a degree in psychology.

After the decision was made to close the school, I applied to schools and was accepted at Boston College. I had no career plans in mind: I only knew that I couldn't teach teenagers for the rest of my life and wanted to work with adult religious, as my friend was doing.

In January 1970, the nuns in Cincinnati had changed from the religious habit to regular clothes, something that was happening in religious orders all over the country. I remember the day I had to go and buy a bra and was humiliated because I couldn't tell the saleslady my size. With my cloistered, habited years, I had lost a sense of some very basic self-knowledge.

In shedding the habit, along with many other religious, I shed the constraints that had been a part of our structured religious life. Clothes, entertainment, and friendships with men—it was as though there was an explosion of repressed adolescence. It was a tumultuous time in religious life and in the country, with the Vietnam War and the civil rights movement calling many things in society into question.

Though marriage still had great appeal for me, and I had several close male friends, I knew that I could find life where I was and that I had to attend to the contemplative dimension of my life. But at times I still cried out angrily, like the prophet Jeremiah, "You have seduced me, and I have let myself be seduced."

Yet I also knew that if I were to leave religious life, it would be because the attractions of the world had blinded me to this part of myself, which, try as I might to deny it, was personally life-affirming. But the "party me" and the "Merton me" still struggled.

In the winter of 1978 one of my colleagues invited me to a party, which coincided with a weekend of solitude I had scheduled. Though I was torn, even then I knew that my conflict was out of proportion to the reality of the two choices. My indecision was rooted in something deeper, which I couldn't identify.

At the recommendation of a spiritual director, I'd been recording my dreams in a journal daily since 1970. In one dream I knew was a turning point even then, I found myself in a large room with French doors looking out to a garden with a huge, bare oak tree. A shadowy figure came from behind the tree and stabbed a priest in the jugular vein. My director of formation came into the community room and told the assembled novices that the priest had been killed.

The next part of the dream consisted of the words *You shall know, even as you are known,* words I later found in Saint Paul's Epistle to the Corinthians. When I woke up, I felt an enormous sense of peace and decided to go to the party. That weekend the blizzard of '78 dropped four feet of snow in the Boston area within twenty-four hours; the party was cancelled. Even though the weather was so inclement that it also impeded travel to the retreat for a weekend of solitude, for me there was enlightenment.

The religious order I belong to was founded in France—hence "French doors"—and was brought to this country by Mother Duchesne, whose last name means "oak" in French. The priest, Father O'Connor, was the director of novices for the Jesuits, an order my brother belonged to for several years before he left and married. With symbols of my religious life in the background, the dream was telling me that I had to actively eliminate the authority figures in my life and that the essence of religious life was in knowing God and being known, not heeding rules and regulations. Though the Voice was beginning to make sense, I still deemed it God's Voice. I remained a work in progress.

At this point in my life, thanks to Russell's insight, I interpret the Voice, along with those that Beth and Taylor heard, as expressions of the deepest part of who we are. Psychology texts describe a "false self," the persona we put on, based on externals: what we have, what we do, who we know, where we go. But this self can be lost when those objects are lost because our identity is bound up with them. The "true self" is at the core of who we are—though we often resist or deny it. Sometimes it is buried beneath illness, layers of abuse, trauma, or the voices of others.

Claiming it was the Voice of God who called me to Kenwood, whom I could persistently blame for my being a nun, meant that I didn't have to own my truest self, the one that found peace and wholeness in a way of life considered odd by worldly standards. Clients besieged by years of illness, having lost a sense of their own strength, can only identify inner voices as those of God, the "other." But this "other" may be the core of who they are—incredibly resilient individuals who need to have someone else hear the inner voice and work with it, no matter what it's named.

In one of my favorite poems, Rilke captures this:

> She who reconciles the ill-matched threads
> of her life, and weaves them gratefully
> into a single cloth—
> it's she who drives the loudmouths from the hall
> and clears it for a different celebration
> where the one guest is you.[1]

Recently I was preparing a presentation for a spirituality conference. The focus was how my work with the men and women in the psychiatric program had changed me, my ideas of God, and the way I pray. As I related this story, I knew in the core of my being that Russell was right. For the first time,

I saw the landscape of my entire journey in a new light. All these years I'd thought the peace I experienced at times of retreat, the contentment I felt in solitude, the centeredness I knew, were respites—spiritual vacations, in a sense—that enabled me to keep going. As I wrote my talk and pondered Russell's words, I owned that like Merton, I was a contemplative. In fact, I was in the right place.

Though I hated statistics when I studied psychology, statistics employed an expression that described the relationship between the formula to be used to analyze the research data and the data itself. "Goodness of fit" meant that you chose the correct formula, neither too sophisticated nor too simple for the data and the hypothesis you proposed. What Russell had captured was that for me there truly was a "goodness of fit" in religious life: I wanted something "other" and had found it there.

I often wonder if I would have ever found the sense of wholeness I know now if I had not entered religious life. At times I can be a materialistic, ambitious, and self-centered person, highly invested in a more superficial sense of myself—what spiritual writers refer to as the "false self." When I am "out in the world" enjoying family, friends, and pleasurable activities, in a way I am always looking over my shoulder, comparing, assessing.

In contrast, when I am with the Beverlys or the Buds, I am among people who have touched their core, though they seldom reflect on it and probably wouldn't even acknowledge it. They know from hard-earned experience what is really of value. With them there is no pretense: what you see is what you get.

At Christmas we often have discussions about gifts. Members of the group are embarrassed because they cannot afford gifts for family members or friends. They want to give "real" gifts, to be able to do what others do with ease. Last Christmas one person sadly said she could only send a card with a very personal message to express her love.

Rather than focusing on material gifts, at Jennifer's suggestion we decided to name a gift each one of us had to offer the world. Once again, the responses were impressive: an ability to listen to others, honesty, compassion, the ability to care and to give love, determination and perseverance, patience.

What was touching about this conversation was the affirmation that each person received when he or she named the gift. Everyone in the group knew these were not just words, that in fact they had witnessed each other listening, caring, being determined and patient, all the more striking because they also know how each one deals with his or her demons.

One of the members ended the discussion on gifts by saying, "Nancy, you are a gift to this group. And you should admit that. You have an ego, too, and you need to accept what you do for us."

Afterward, thinking of her response, I thought of how difficult it is for me to own some of my own gifts. I recalled a line from our religious rule:

> Humility requires further that they should never quit the
> thought of their own lowliness and nothingness, that they
> should accept with a certain satisfaction the contempt and
> humiliations which Divine Providence may deign to provide
> for them, and that when success is granted to their labors, they
> should refer all the glory thereof faithfully to the Heart of Jesus,
> the source of every good.[2]

As nuns-in-training, we had to memorize the rulebook, and we heard this passage read aloud once a month. From the ages of eighteen to twenty-one, I heard that I should never forget my lowliness and nothingness, not that I was a gifted, personable, attractive, engaging, intelligent woman. Not only did we have lines like these to memorize, but we also examined our conscience twice a day. We never focused on the good we had done or the gifts we had received from God, from others, or from life but rather on what we had failed to do or be. And we certainly were not to shine in any way.

One year during my checkered career as a teacher, the director of the school's drama department quit during the second semester of the academic year. Because I was only teaching second grade and had no other time-consuming responsibilities, the principal asked me to take over. Though I'd been in plays in high school, I knew nothing about directing, but I obediently said yes. For days I read books on how to direct a play.

The senior class that year was a particularly challenging group of young women. They were insulted that a mere second-grade teacher was going to direct their class production. One late afternoon, quaking in my black nun's shoes, I confronted the ringleader of the group and said, "Whether you like it or not, I am the director, so you had better make up your mind to go along with me, or this play won't happen at all." From then on, we worked together and put on a smashing performance of *Pride and Prejudice*.

The night of the final show, when the cast members were taking their bows, I had been instructed by the superior not to appear on stage, to receive flowers, or in any way accept any accolades for my part in the performance. I was crushed. I had worked so hard; I had overcome so many obstacles to do the play. I really wanted to take a bow and hear the applause, an antidote to the criticism to which I had become so accustomed.

What would have happened if I had taken a bow, if I had been able to acknowledge to myself that I had been a gift to that group of high school seniors?

Over the years, though many people have told me how gifted I am, it is not part of the reality I live with. No matter how many lists of my good qualities I've received from various nominations in my religious order or how many excellent evaluations I've gotten from programs I've done, I still look at myself through the lens of "not yet, not enough." If I have such a hard time affirming myself, even with all my advantages, how much more difficult, and at the same wonderful, it is when the men and women in the groups can name the ways in which they are a gift to the world after years of seeing themselves as psychiatric patients? *I am patient; I have compassion; I am a good listener.*

In the mental health world, we use descriptions like "higher-functioning" to identify people, as opposed to "lower-functioning." The reality is that most of the men and women I know function at a higher level than I do most of the time because they have so many more daily barriers to overcome. Mental illness is like an albatross; like Sisyphus, they labor under an enormous rock. They seldom look in the mirror and say, *What a strong person I am* or *How wonderful that I can be honest, caring, and compassionate as I struggle with this weight on my back.*

These men and women have been a gift to me, as I have been to them. They have held up a mirror and allowed me to see a different image of myself, and I, in turn, have done the same for them.

On a cold, snowy day, the daughter of a friend of mine insisted on wearing her patent leather shoes to day care. Wisely, the child said that her mother could carry her to the car, and her mother agreed, saying, "I like holding you."

Rebecca, the daughter, replied, "We're like mirrors: you like to hold me, and I like to be holded."

I may not have my own Rebecca, but I have had Beverly, Bud, Jennifer, Andrea, Beth, Jim, Russell, and all the others. When they look at the mirror I hold up to them, they see signs of life, creative spirits, value, compassion, and resilience. In the mirror they hold up to me, I have begun to see not a barren desert but a flowering landscape.

Epilogue

I love to travel, but for me the preparations and the process of getting to my destination and the people I meet along the way have always been more exciting and adventuresome than arriving at my final destination. It is the unknown, the frequent need to adapt, the aspects of myself that I discover in the process that make the trip worthwhile and that stay with me long after the journey.

So it has been with this book, which has captured the process I have been involved in since I said yes to that Voice more than fifty years ago and to the phone call that started the journey within the journey. Numerous times since I began my work in the day treatment program, I have been invited to take a different path, to take on administrative roles in my religious order. I always said no, based on an intuition that I had something to contribute to the dialogue between mental illness and faith.

I see now that this book has become that contribution, but what I could never have imagined is that my attentive listening to and struggling with my inner angel, the one that kept calling me into the unknown, would, even when I resisted it, lead me and the people I have had the privilege of working with to a new sense of life. Since the day Russell said, "Maybe that was the deepest part of *you*," I have continued to know a sense of peace and rightness about who I am and where I am.

The image that comes to mind is a puzzle. The men and women I have worked with have filled in some of the pieces in my puzzle, just as I have helped them put in place some of the pieces in their puzzles. When the process of writing this book became overwhelming and discouraging and I couldn't see where the road was taking me, it was the voices and the presence of the clients, their interest in the book, and my deep commitment and connection to them that kept me on the journey. I was tied to them as the little children to the ropes, and together we have been on quite a voyage.

My father was right when he said, "Life is a learning process." And my mother was too when she said, "Life is about loving, being grateful, and making a contribution."

Appendix

RELIGIOUS HISTORY QUESTIONNAIRE

Asurvey conducted by the Pew Forum on Religion and Public Life in February 2008 revealed a curious phenomenon in the religious affiliation of Americans: 44 percent of American adults have left the denomination of their childhood for another denomination, adopted a different a spiritual path, or are disaffiliated entirely. Although a religious affiliation or spiritual practice of some kind is important to a large percentage of Americans (78.4 percent say they are Christian and 4.7 percent cite other religious traditions), mental health providers, as indicated in this book, do not always explore this aspect of a person's life.

The following religious history questionnaire was originally intended for use in the context of mental health treatment, not in its entirety but more as a guide, suggesting to the therapist areas to explore in order to understand the positive or negative aspects of a person's religious experience. Although a person may define himself or herself as spiritual and not religious, he or she may have some unresolved issues related to religion. Hence further inquiry may reveal important personal history for the therapeutic work.

Since our experience of religion is intertwined with our family history, our personal development, and even our social context, anyone who reads this book may benefit from reflecting on some of these questions. This may be done in a variety of ways.

Using some of the questions as a guide, journaling about our memories and experiences in a religious tradition at different stages of our development may reveal both hidden treasures and possibly some land mines that have been buried for years but that nonetheless affect us.

In my clinical experience I have observed that couples, either before or after marriage, frequently avoid the discussion of their religious, spiritual, or faith experiences. As with the issue of money, the details are not explored. Knowing more about a person's religious past can deepen the relationship and also be a guide in thinking about how children are to be raised.

If this book is read in a book club, having a conversation with the group about each person's religious experience can be enlightening and freeing. Even when individuals have been raised in the same religious tradition, such as Jewish, Roman Catholic, Evangelical, or Muslim, individual differences exist because of socioeconomic, familial, and educational influences. Working with the questionnaire in a group also liberates us from preconceived notions we have about different traditions.

Individuals who do hospice work or work with terminally ill patients or the elderly may also benefit from exploring some of these questions. At no time in one's life is it more important to name how one sees God, a Higher Power, or the absence of anything after death, as well as dealing with issues of reconciliation, fear, guilt, or despair.

My references to *religion* or *religiosity* are to an organized system of beliefs that are expressed by and within a community with a structure that includes authority figures, rituals, rules, and a tradition that is both oral and written. The word *spirituality* is more difficult to define but may include one or more of the following:

- Personal beliefs and practices
- The transcendent dimension of life and existence, the "other," the sacred
- One's ultimate values
- A sense of wholeness
- A sense of meaning and purpose
- Whatever gives hope or brings peace
- Faith in something
- A sense of belonging or connection with something beyond the self
- Blessing, goodness, how we treat ourselves and others
- Reverence and respect for life, one's own and that of others
- An inner life

Whether we grew up in a religious tradition or not, we have all been shaped by a consciousness of religion. Knowing what has influenced us and understanding how others have been formed by their traditions may lead to more personal freedom and lessening of prejudice.

Religious/Spiritual History Assessment

Exploration Related to Family of Origin

1. Were you raised in a religious tradition? If so, which one?

If answer is no, go to question 2.
If answer is yes:

    a. How would you describe your family's involvement in religion? Did your parents and grandparents follow the same tradition?

b. Who was the most responsible for encouraging religious practices or communicating religious messages?

c. What were some of the religious practices or messages that most affected you, either positively or negatively?

d. Was attendance at religious services frequent or infrequent, mandatory or voluntary?

e. Who in your family attended religious services?

f. Did your family refer to God, a Higher Power, or a Supreme Being? If so, in what ways?

g. In a crisis, did your family rely on God, a Higher Power, or a Supreme Being? In what ways?

h. What was your family's contact with religious professionals (rabbis, priests, nuns, ministers, and similar)?

i. In the social context in which you were raised, was a religious affiliation viewed positively or negatively?

2. Were you raised in a spiritual tradition?

a. How would you describe your family's involvement in its spiritual tradition?

b. Who encouraged spiritual practice?

c. What did the practice consist of?

d. In a crisis, did your family rely on spiritual practices or beliefs?

If you responded no to questions 1 and 2:

3. What was your family's view of religion or people who had religious faith or a spiritual practice?

Exploration Related to Developmental Stages

Ages 3–12

+ What is your earliest memory of any experience or event that you might describe as spiritual or religious?

- As a young child, did you think about God, a Higher Power, or a Supreme Being? Can you describe how you imagined that Being?

- Did anyone close to you die, a person or a pet? Between the ages of three and seven, did you ever think about what happened to people or pets when they died?

- Did the adults talk about the death? What do you remember about that?

- Did you say prayers? If so, to whom, how, and for what? What was the "pattern" (every night, at meals, and so on)? Who taught you to pray?

- Was your elementary school education in a religious school? What was that like for you?

- If not, did you attend religious classes after public school?

- If you did not attend a religious school, did your friends? Were you aware of this? What was that like for you?

- If you attended religious services, what did you like most, and what did you like least?

- Was there any religious person who was important to you?

- When did God or a Spiritual Being feel closest, and when farthest away?

- Was there consistency or inconsistency between what you observed in your family and religious messages that you heard at home, in school, in your religious group, or elsewhere?

- If you experienced a crisis during this time in your life, did any religious practice, clergyperson, or institution help you? Did any nonreligious practice help you?

Ages 12–18

- As a teenager, did you feel a conflict related to sexual feelings, desires, fantasies, and your faith or religious belief? If you did, how did you cope with the conflict?

+ Did you receive religious instruction during your teenage years?
+ If you attended religious services, what was that like for you?
+ Was there any clergyperson who was important to you? Who was it, and what made the person important to you?
+ When did God or a Spiritual Being feel closest and when farthest away?
+ Did you pray or meditate? If so, to whom and for what? Was there a pattern to your prayer or meditation?
+ Have you ever had a significant religious or spiritual experience that you believe changed your life? Would you describe that for me?
+ When you were in distress (afraid, alone, in danger, or the like), were your beliefs a support to you, a burden, or irrelevant?

Ages 18–25

+ During this period of your life, were there changes in your religious tradition or spiritual practice?
+ If so, what changed, and how did the changes occur?
+ Did your religious beliefs affect you in terms of dating or sexual relationships or behavior?
+ Were you married in a religious ceremony? If you were, was it your choice, your family's, or your spouse's? Is or was marrying someone of the same faith important to you?
+ What family expectations did you encounter if you decided to change traditions?

Ages 25–65

+ Are you still active in your original religious tradition?

If answer is yes:

+ What is that like for you now?

If answer is no:

+ At what point in your life did that change?
+ Would you say that you have a spiritual life? How would you describe that?
+ Do you and your spouse or partner belong to the same religious tradition or have similar spiritual practices?
+ How would you describe your image of God or a Higher Power at this point in your life?
+ Did becoming a parent make a difference in the way you thought about belonging to a religious tradition or engaging in a spiritual practice?
+ If you raised your children in a religious tradition, do they still practice in that tradition, or have they changed to another? If they have changed, how has that affected you?
+ At a time of crisis, are your beliefs a source of comfort for you or a conflict?

Ages 65 and Over

+ As you age, are your religious beliefs a source of comfort to you, a source of distress, or irrelevant?
+ Hope, forgiveness, loss, diminishment, death, and afterlife are major concerns of people as they age. If you belong to a religious tradition or have a spiritual practice, does this assist or support you with these issues?
+ Have your religious beliefs provided a sense of meaning for you as you reflect on your life?
+ If you do not have a religious tradition or spiritual practice, what has provided you with a sense of meaning?

Notes

Prologue

1. Koenig, H., ed. *Handbook of Religion and Mental Health*. San Diego, Calif.: Academic Press, 1998.
2. Rizzuto, A.-M. *The Birth of the Living God: A Psychoanalytic Study*. Chicago: University of Chicago Press, 1979.
3. Bergin, A. E., and Jensen, J. P. "Religiosity of Psychotherapists: A National Survey." *Psychotherapy*, 1990, 27, 3–7.
4. Waldfogel, S., Wolpe, P., and Shmuely, Y. "Religious Training and Religiosity in Psychiatric Residency Programs." *Academic Psychiatry*, 1998, 22, 29–35.

Chapter 1: Exploring New Terrain

1. Over the years I have led four groups. For the sake of simplicity, I make reference to one group, although the material in this book was derived from all four groups.

Chapter 2: Beverly's Quest

1. Electroconvulsive therapy, also known as electroshock therapy, involves applying an electric current to the head to induce convulsions and unconsciousness; it is still in occasional use today. Insulin shock therapy, used in the 1950s and 1960s, was a psychiatric treatment in which patients were injected with large doses of insulin to produce a daily coma over the course of several weeks.

2. Borderline personality disorder is a psychiatric diagnosis characterized by impulsivity, anger, and self-destructive behavior but only brief psychotic episodes, if any.

3. Eliot, T. S. "East Coker." In *The Complete Poems and Plays*. New York: Harcourt Brace, 1971, pp. 126–127. Originally published 1940.

Chapter 3: Creative Spirits

1. Hopkins, G. M. "God's Grandeur." In *Poems and Prose*, ed. W. N. Gardner. Oxford: Oxford University Press, 1963, p. 27. Originally published 1918.

2. Rilke, R. M. "God Speaks to Each of Us." In *Rilke's Book of Hours: Love Poems to God*, trans. A. Barrows and J. Macy. New York: Riverhead Books, 1996, p. 119.

Chapter 4: Buddy, an Unlikely Prophet

1. Eliot, T. S. "Dry Salvages." In *The Complete Poems and Plays*. New York: Harcourt Brace, 1971, p. 133.

2. Heschel, A. *The Prophets*. New York: HarperCollins, 1962.

Chapter 5: The Role of Ritual in Healing

1. Frankl, V. *Man's Search for Meaning*. New York: Washington Square Press, 1963, pp. 178–179.

2. Cooper, S. "The Shortest Day" (poem written for Christmas Revels). Brooklyn, N.Y.: New York Revels, 1977.

Chapter 6: The Dilemma of Voices

1. Albom, M. *Tuesdays with Morrie: An Old Man, a Young Man, and Life's Greatest Lesson*. New York: Doubleday, 1997, p. 163.

2. James, W. *The Varieties of Religious Experience*. New York: New American Library, 1958, p. 34. Originally published 1902.

3. Julian of Norwich. *The Revelations of Divine Love*, trans. J. Walsh. Saint Meinrad, Ind.: Abbey Press, 1974, p. 91.

Chapter 7: Wrestling with God

1. Rilke, R. M. "She Who Reconciles the Ill-Matched Threads." In *Rilke's Book of Hours: Love Poems to God*, trans. A. Barrows and J. Macy. New York: Riverhead Books, 1996, p. 119.

2. *Constitution and Rules of the Society of the Sacred Heart*, rev. 1922, p. 46.

The Author

Nancy Kehoe, R.S.C.J., Ph.D., is a member of the Religious of the Sacred Heart. She is a clinical instructor in psychology in the Department of Psychiatry at the Cambridge Health Alliance, affiliated with Harvard Medical School, a position she has held since 1980. Her area of expertise is religion and spirituality in the clinical context. For twenty-seven years, using a model she created, she has led groups on spiritual beliefs and values for adults with psychiatric disabilities. She currently consults with health care providers in mental health and geriatric settings, teaching them how to address the religious and spiritual needs of individuals. She has presented at regional, national, and international conferences and published on the subject of religion and psychotherapy.

Additional information can be found on her Web site: http://www.expandingconnections.com.

Index

This page is a continuation of the copyright page.

"God Speaks to each of us . . ."; "She who reconciles . . . ," from RILKE'S BOOK OF HOURS: LOVE POEMS TO GOD by Rainer Maria Rilke, translated by Anita Barrows and Joanna Macy. Copyright © 1996 by Anita Barrows and Joanna Macy. Originally published in Riverhead Books. Reprinted by permission of the translators.

"Gott spricht zu jedem . . . /God speaks to each of us . . ."; "Wer seines Lebens viele Widersinne/She who reconciles . . . ," from RILKE'S BOOK OF HOURS: LOVE POEMS TO GOD by Rainer Maria Rilke, translated by Anita Barrows and Joanna Macy. Copyright © 1996 Anita Barrows and Joanna Macy. Used by permission of Riverhead Books, an imprint of Penguin Group (USA) Inc.

Excerpt from "The Dry Salvages" in FOUR QUARTERS, copyright 1941 by T. S. Eliot and renewed 1969 by Esme Valerie Eliot, reprinted by permission of Houghton Mifflin Harcourt Publishing Company. Used by permission of Faber and Faber Ltd.

Excerpt from "East Coker" in FOUR QUARTERS, copyright 1940 by T. S. Eliot and renewed 1968 by Esme Valerie Eliot, reprinted by permission of Houghton Mifflin Harcourt Publishing Company. Used by permission of Faber and Faber Ltd.

God's Grandeur from "Poems and Prose" by Hopkins GM edited by Garner WN (1963). Used by permission of Oxford University Press on behalf of the British Province of the Society of Jesus.

Excerpt from The Shortest Day, © Susan Cooper. Written in 1977 for The Christmas Revels®. Used with permission Revels, Inc.

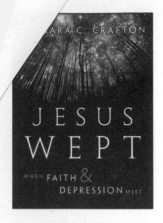

JESUS WEPT

When Faith and Depression Meet

Barbara C. Crafton

ISBN 978-0-470-37195-4
Hardcover | 192 pp.

"...Barbara Crafton offers up her truth with humor and gritty stories as well as candor and care. Despite our growing openness about depression, shame is still its frequent companion. May the many who suffer from this death-in-life, and those who care for them, read this book, shed the shame, and find the new life that awaits them on the other side." —**Parker J. Palmer**, author of *A Hidden Wholeness* and *Let Your Life Speak*

In the first book to discuss depression from a faith perspective, Barbara Crafton expertly weaves personal stories and helpful resources to explore depression as it is affected (for both better and worse) by Christian faith. She contends that it is harder for people of faith to come to terms with depression since they may attribute its causes to something they have done, rather than to its true root in physiology and genetics.

This is a book people will want to buy for themselves and give to loved ones who are suffering from depression and wondering where God is during their pain and anguish.

Barbara C. Crafton (Metuchen, NJ) is an Episcopal priest, spiritual director, and author. She is the founder and head of the Geranium Farm (geraniumfarm.org), an online institute for the promotion of spiritual growth.